The

CASE

PAST, PRESENT, AND FUTURE

FOR

BOOKS

With a New Chapter on Google
and the Digital Future

ROBERT DARNTON

Praise for
Robert Darnton and *The Case for Books*

"Robert Darnton's essays collected in *The Case for Books* should be read not only by those concerned at the technological threat to the printed page but by all the younger 'digital natives who know "text" primarily as a verb.' Thus does H. J. Jackson begin her review of a nuanced and subtle collection which, while addressing anxieties about the present and future of Google, is less alarmist than others of the older generation have been." —*Times Literary Supplement*

"[A] fascinating history of our literary past and a penetrating look at the disruptive forces shaping the future of publishing. Almost no topic is untouched, from the role of libraries to metadata, the print traditions of Europe, piracy old and new, Darnton's own forays into digital initiatives, and the efficacy— even the beauty—of our changing literary landscape over centuries of development . . . the book offers a deep dive into the evolution of the written and published word." —*Publishers Weekly*

"Historian and library director Darnton has written expansively and lucidly on the history of books and libraries. This collection of his influential essays from the past decade neatly encapsulates one significant part of his immense legacy and contribution to intellectual history. . . . Every one of Darnton's essays reflects both his erudition and his good humor." —*Booklist*

"Neither jeremiad nor rant, this eloquent gem by the world's premier historian of the book is an exploration of how print can flourish in the digital world. Robert Darnton, director of the Harvard University Library and founder of the Gutenberg-e online book program, explains how books are parts of 'circuits of information' and that 'historians can show that books do not merely recount history; they make it.' Rather than deploring the (exaggerated) demise of the book, we need to understand how all of us in the world of communication, from the librarians, publishers, computer engineers, and webmasters to readers, can make it together through the thickets of the information landscape."

—Editor's Choice, *Chicago Tribune*

"Darnton knows this territory as well as anyone and views the subject from a unique perspective . . . The stimulating and thought-provoking essays in *The Case for Books: Past, Present, and Future* provide us with an excellent overview of where we have been and where we are likely to be headed . . . Darnton's thoughtful and incisive essays on this important topic should be of interest to a wide range of book lovers."

—*BookPage*

"In this collection of well-informed essays, Robert Darnton, historian and director of the Harvard University Library, offers a decidedly open-minded perspective on some of the technological changes affecting the world of books and leads an insightful and learned discussion of topics that will appeal to more traditional bibliophiles." —*Shelf Awareness*

"Darnton's book ticks all the boxes. It looks nice. It smells nice. Its content is intelligent and forms a valuable primer to an increasingly important debate." —*The Scotsman*

"[Darnton has] applied a masterly eye for detail, condensing a history of books into enlightening insights about where we may find the book—in its many forms—in the future."

—*Star Tribune*

THE CASE FOR BOOKS

The
Case *for* Books

Past, Present, and Future

ROBERT DARNTON

PUBLICAFFAIRS
New York

PublicAffairs books are available at special discounts for bulk purchases in the United States by corporations, institutions, and other organizations. For more information, please contact the Special Markets Department at the Perseus Books Group, 2300 Chestnut Street, Suite 200, Philadelphia, PA 19103, or call (800) 810-4145, ext. 5000, or e-mail special.markets@perseusbooks.com.

The essays in this book appeared under different titles in various publications. In order to avoid repetition, they have been cut and modified in some places. The originals can be found in the following sources: Chapter 1, "Google and the Future of Books" in the *New York Review of Books*, February 12, 2009, pp. 9–11. Chapter 2, "The Library in the New Age" in the *New York Review of Books*, June 12, 2008, pp. 72–80. Chapter 3, a lecture given at the Frankfurt Book Fair on October 17, 2009. Chapter 4, "Lost and Found in Cyberspace" in the *Chronicle of Higher Education*, March 12, 1999, pp. 134–135. Chapter 5, "The New Age of the Book" in the *New York Review of Books*, March 18, 1999, pp. 5–7. Chapter 6, a grant application and report sent to the Andrew W. Mellon Foundation in 1997 and 2002. Chapter 7, an op-ed essay in the *Harvard Crimson*, February 12, 2008. Chapter 8, "The Great Book Massacre" in the *New York Review of Books*, April 26, 2001, pp. 16–19. Chapter 9, "The Heresies of Bibliography" in the *New York Review of Books*, May 29, 2003, pp. 43–45. Chapter 10, "Extraordinary Commonplaces" in the *New York Review of Books*, December 21, 2000, pp. 82–87. Chapter 11, "What Is the History of Books?" in *Daedalus,* summer 1982, pp. 65–83.

Designed by Brent Wilcox

A CIP catalog record is available for this book from the Library of Congress.
Hardcover ISBN-13: 978-1-586-48826-0
Paperback ISBN: 978-1-586-48902-1

10 9 8 7 6 5 4 3 2

CONTENTS

PART III
Past

INTRODUCTION

This is a book about books, an unashamed apology for the printed word, past, present, and future. It is also an argument about the place of books in the digital environment that has now become a fundamental fact of life for millions of human beings. Far from deploring electronic modes of communication, I want to explore the possibilities of aligning them with the power that Johannes Gutenberg unleashed more than five centuries ago. What common ground exists between old books and e-books? What mutual advantages link libraries with the Internet? Those questions may sound empty in the abstract, but they take concrete form in decisions made every day by players in the communication industry—webmasters, computer engineers, financiers, lawyers, publishers, librarians, and a great many ordinary readers.

Having played a bit part myself, I offer this collection of essays for whatever help it may provide to anyone attempting to find a way through the information landscape. My own way led through a great deal of unfamiliar territory. After a brief career as a reporter, mainly covering crime for the *Newark Star Ledger* and the *New York Times*, I became a college professor and spent most of my time in the eighteenth century, studying a subject that came to be known as the history of books. Research on publishing in the age of Enlightenment led to an opportunity to observe publishers at work in the modern world, when I spent four years on the editorial board of the Princeton University Press and then fifteen years as a trustee of the Oxford University Press (USA). The OUP's headquarters on Madison Avenue provided a view of the trade as well as the academic side of publishing. A summer as a scholar in residence at the CBS network opened up another view from a corporate office high up on Sixth Avenue. Election to the board of trustees of the New York Public Library brought me back to the heart of book country at Fifth Avenue and Forty-second Street. By then I was publishing trade books at W. W. Norton a block away and articles with the *New York Review of Books* across town at Broadway and Fifty-seventh Street. I could not have followed a more revealing itinerary through the contemporary world of books, had I planned it in advance. But it all happened by improvisation and good luck, as occasions arose.

Along the way, I helped launch two publishing ventures of my own design: the Electronic Enlightenment, a digital database formed from the correspondence of Voltaire, Rousseau, Franklin, and Jefferson (it is now being sold by the Voltaire Foundation of Oxford as a subscription package whose contents differ somewhat from what I had originally envisioned), and Gutenberg-e, a series of electronic monographs produced from prize-winning dissertations in history (they, too, were sold as subscriptions by the publisher, the Columbia University Press). The Andrew W. Mellon Foundation financed both projects and helped me learn something about the importance of business plans and the possibility of promoting the public good from initiatives in the private sector.

Finally, I set out to write a large-scale e-book about publishing and the book trade in eighteenth-century Europe. But before I built a Web site, I received an unexpected phone call from the provost of Harvard University: would I be willing to be considered for an appointment as the next director of the Harvard University Library? I did not hesitate long before saying yes. Here was an opportunity to do something about the issues I had studied as historical phenomena. The job did not in principle involve a heavy load of administration. On the contrary, I was expected to continue research and teaching as a university professor while leaving the management of the libraries (estimates of their number varied from 40 to 104, depending on definitions of a library) to the head librarians, who are generally recognized as the best in the profession. But in July 2007, as soon as I moved into my office, I learned that Harvard was involved in secret talks with Google about a project that took my breath away. Google planned to digitize millions of books, beginning with those at Harvard and three other university libraries, and to market the digital copies, drawing on a database that would become the world's greatest library, bigger by far than anything dreamt of since the library of Alexandria.

Google Book Search, as it came to be known, developed from an attempt to settle a lawsuit against Google in September and October 2005 by a group of authors and publishers who claimed that by digitizing books from research libraries and displaying snippets from them on the Web, Google was infringing copyright. Harvard had no part in the suit, but it had to be informed about the negotiations for a settlement, because Google Book Search would never get off the ground if it did not win the cooperation of the libraries that would supply the books for digitization. I spent a large proportion of my first two years at Harvard huddling with lawyers and struggling to understand the implications of the settlement as it was gradually hammered out. Everything had to be kept secret, owing to nondisclosure agreements, until the settlement was made public on October 28, 2008. By then I had received something of an education in the ways of corporate litigation and the strange world of Google, where young engineers sat around on inflated rubber balls dreaming up algorithms that could lead a search for anything. (During one visit to a Google office, I asked an insider how he would describe the status hierarchy of the company. "Easy," he replied. "First come the engineers, then the lawyers, then the chefs.")

Dazzled as I was by the vision of a digital mega-library, I had doubts about letting Harvard's collections of books, built up at enormous effort and expense since 1638, become part of a commercial speculation. I did not object to Google's project of making books in the public domain available free of charge on the Internet, but Google planned to sell subscriptions to the digitized database, composed of books protected by copyright, and to share the proceeds with the plaintiffs who were suing the company. The more I learned about Google, the more it appeared to be a monopoly intent on conquering markets rather than a natural ally of libraries, whose sole purpose is to preserve and diffuse knowledge. I tried to explain the issues posed by Google Book Search in two articles published in the *New York Review of Books* and reprinted here. Since then a lively public debate has developed, and it is still going strong as I write, when the fate of the settlement remains to be determined by a court, which will begin to deliberate on October 7, 2009.

The other issue that occupied me heavily during my first two years at Harvard was a local version of the general movement known as open access. In collaboration with Stuart Shieber, a computer scientist committed to the open-access cause, and with the support of Harvard's provost, Steven Hyman, I defended a motion before the Faculty of Arts and Sciences to make all scholarly articles by members of the faculty available online and free of charge. The motion was carried unanimously on February 12, 2008. Since then, similar motions have been adopted by the Law School, the Kennedy School of Government, and the School of Education. The other schools that together make up Harvard University are expected to follow suit, so that a "Harvard model" for open access is being debated widely in the academic world. What distinguishes it from other open-access policies is its mandatory character. Faculty members are required to transfer a nonexclusive license to Harvard, making their scholarship freely accessible from a repository, which the library administers through the Office for Scholarly Communication. They can opt out by obtaining a waiver, which is granted automatically, but they are committed in principle to communicating the results of their research openly to anyone with Internet access.

The principle of openness underlies several other projects discussed in the following essays. I do not expect my readers to have any particular interest in the goings-on at Harvard, but Harvard's library, as it happens, provides an ideal site for dealing with the problems that exist everywhere in the world of learning—problems of paying for the exorbitant costs of journals, of preserving texts "born digital," of defending fair use in assigning texts to students, of including Web sites and e-mail among the sources saved for future research. There are practical problems, too. How to keep up with acquiring printed books while advancing on the digital front? How to develop a new business model that will free scholarly journals from the commercial speculations of publishers? How to legitimize electronic monographs in the eyes of conservatives who believe that a book can exist only in print? The questions open onto the entire future of communication. I hope they will interest a broad readership, even if I present them as they appeared to me in my small corner of a college campus.

Any attempt to see into the future while struggling with problems in the present should be informed, I believe, by studying the past. I have therefore organized this collection of essays in three sections, running backward from speculations about the world of books that will exist in five or ten years to polemics about issues in the here-and-now and reflections on older information ages with communication systems of their own. Not that the essays were meant to fit in any prefabricated structure. They were written as occasions arose and fired off, scattershot, at moving targets.

If I may switch metaphors, I would argue that an essay can be used to assay a subject, somewhat as metallurgists do when they drill into a substance to test its composition. Review essays are especially useful in this respect. The final section of this book contains three review essays that I wrote to examine different aspects of book history: paper, the basic material of literature from the fifteenth to the twenty-first century; bibliography, the principal tool for taking the measure of texts; and reading, the most fundamental and mysterious element in the communication process. Communication itself—the notion of interrelated stages in producing and consuming books—is the subject of the last chapter, which attempts to characterize the history of books in general and to illustrate its methods by drawing on archival research. I believe that book history is one of the most vital fields in the humanities. Does its success express a fascination for a world we have lost now that the Internet makes the printing press look archaic?

Perhaps, but the study of books need not be limited to a particular technology. In working back into the historical dimension of my subject, I hope to help the reader take a long-term view of current problems. Although the study of history does not, in my opinion, afford lessons that can be directly applied to present circumstances, immersion in the past can provide a useful perspective on current and future events. People today feel the ground shifting beneath their feet, tipping toward a new era that will be determined by innovations in technology. We see the change in patterns of behavior. A generation "born digital" is "always on," conversing everywhere on cell phones, tapping out instant messages, and networking in actual or virtual realities. The younger people you pass on the street or sit next to on a bus are simultaneously there and not there. They shake their shoulders and tap their feet to music audible only to them inside the cocoon of their digital systems. They seem to be wired differently from their elders, whose orientation to machines comes from another zone of the subconscious. Older generations learned to adjust dials by turning knobs; younger generations toggle. The difference between turning and toggling may seem trivial, but it derives from reflexes situated deep in the kinetic memory. We find our way through the world by means of a sensory disposition that the Germans call *Fingerspitzengefühl*. If you were trained to guide a pen with your index finger, look at the way young people use their thumbs on mobile phones, and you will see how technology penetrates a new generation, body and soul.

Does the change in *Fingerspitzengefühl* mean that readers soon will cease to thumb through books? It seems that reading machines have won a place in the information landscape. But the oldest machine of all, the codex, continues to dominate the market for reading matter. In fact, its market share is actually increasing. According to *Bowker's Global Books in Print*, 700,000 new titles appeared worldwide in 1998; 859,000 in 2003; and 976,000 in 2007. Despite the current downturn of the economy, soon a million new books will be published every year.

The staying power of the old-fashioned codex illustrates a general principle in the history of communication: one medium does not displace another, at least not in the short run. Manuscript publishing flourished long after Gutenberg's invention; newspapers did not wipe out the printed book; the radio did not replace the newspaper; television did not destroy the radio; and the Internet did not make viewers abandon their television sets. Does technological change therefore offer a reassuring message about continuity, despite the proliferation of new inventions?

No. The explosion of electronic modes of communication is as revolutionary as the invention of printing with movable type, and we are having as much difficulty in assimilating it as readers did in the fifteenth century, when they confronted printed texts. Here, for example, is a letter by Niccolò Perotti, a learned Italian classicist, to Francesco Guarnerio, written in 1471, less than twenty years after Gutenberg's invention:

> My dear Francesco, I have lately kept praising the age in which we live, because of the great, indeed divine gift of the new kind of writing which was recently brought to us from Germany. In fact, I saw a single man printing in a single month as much as could be written by hand by several persons in a year. . . . It was for this reason that I was led to hope that within a short time we should have such a large quantity of books that there wouldn't be a single work which could not be procured because of lack of

means or scarcity. . . . Yet—oh false and all too human thoughts—I see that things turned out quite differently from what I had hoped. Because now that anyone is free to print whatever they wish, they often disregard that which is best and instead write, merely for the sake of entertainment, what would best be forgotten, or, better still be *erased* from all books. And even when they write something worthwhile they twist it and corrupt it to the point where it would be much better to do without such books, rather than having a thousand copies spreading falsehoods over the whole world.*

Perotti sounds like some of the critics of Google Book Search, myself included, who regret the textual imperfections and bibliographical inexactitudes in the "new kind of writing" brought to us over the Internet. Whatever the future may be, it will be digital. The present is a time of transition, when printed and digital modes of communication coexist and new technology soon becomes obsolete. Already we are witnessing the disappearance of familiar objects: the typewriter, now consigned to antique shops; the postcard, a curiosity; the handwritten letter, beyond the capacity of most young people, who cannot write in cursive script; the daily newspaper, extinct in many cities; the local bookshop, replaced by chains, which themselves are threatened by Internet distributors like Amazon. And the library?

It can look like the most archaic institution of all. Yet its past bodes well for its future, because libraries were never warehouses of books. They have always been and always will be centers of learning. Their central position in the world of

*I would like to thank Bernard Rosenthal for the translation of this passage, which he kindly sent to me.

learning makes them ideally suited to mediate between the printed and the digital modes of communication. Books, too, can accommodate both modes. Whether printed on paper or stored in servers, they embody knowledge, and their authority derives from a great deal more than the technology that went into them. They owe some of their authority to authors, although they commanded respect long before the cult of the author took shape in the eighteenth century. As book historians insist, authors write texts, but books are made by book professionals, and the professionals exercise functions that extend far beyond manufacturing and diffusing a product. Publishers are gatekeepers, who control the flow of knowledge. From the boundless variety of matter susceptible to being made public, they select what they think will sell or should be sold, according to their professional expertise and their personal convictions. Publishers' judgments, informed by long experience in the marketplace of ideas, determines what reaches readers, and readers need to rely on it more than ever in an age of information overload. By selecting texts, editing them, designing them to be readable, and bringing them to the attention of readers, book professionals provide services that will outlast all changes in technology.

I am pleased, therefore, to offer these essays in codex form as words printed on paper, and I am happy that my publisher, PublicAffairs, will also make them available on the Internet and in audio recordings. Most of the essays appeared originally in the *New York Review of Books*, whose editor, Robert Silvers, has corrected my prose and sharpened my thoughts for nearly forty years. I would like to express my gratitude to him and to Peter Osnos and Clive Priddle at PublicAffairs, whose expertise was crucial in transforming these essays into a book.

GOOGLE AND THE NEW DIGITAL FUTURE

November 9 is one of those strange dates haunted by history. On November 9, 1989, the Berlin Wall fell, signaling the collapse of the Soviet empire. The Nazis organized *Kristallnacht* on November 9, 1938, beginning their all-out campaign against Jews. On November 9, 1923, Hitler's Beer Hall Putsch was crushed in Munich, and on November 9, 1918, Kaiser Wilhelm II abdicated and Germany was declared a republic. The date especially hovers over the history of Germany, but it marks great events in other countries as well: the Meiji Restoration in Japan, November 9, 1867; Bonaparte's coup effectively ending the French Revolution, November 9, 1799; and the first sighting of land by the Pilgrims on the *Mayflower*, November 9, 1620.

On November 9, 2009, in the district court for the Southern District of New York, the Authors Guild and the Association of American Publishers were scheduled to file a settlement to resolve their suit against Google. The suit was for alleged breach of copyright in its program to digitize millions of books from research libraries and to make them available, for a fee, online. Not comparable to the fall of the Berlin Wall, you might say. True, but for several months, all eyes in the world of books—

authors, publishers, librarians, and a great many readers—were trained on the district court and its judge, Denny Chin, because this seemingly small-scale squabble over copyright looked likely to determine the digital future for all of us.

Google has by now digitized some 10 million books. On what terms will it make those texts available to readers? That is the question before Judge Chin. If he construes the case narrowly, according to precedents in class-action suits, he could conclude that none of the parties had been slighted. That decision would remove all obstacles to Google's attempt to transform its digitizing into the largest library and bookselling business the world has ever known. If Judge Chin were to take a broad view of the case, the settlement could be modified in ways that would protect the public against potential abuses of Google's monopolistic power.

That Google's enterprise (Google Book Search or GBS) threatened to become an overweening monopoly became clear when the Department of Justice filed a memorandum with the court warning about the likelihood of a violation of antitrust legislation. More than 400 other memorandums and amicus briefs also provided warning signals about mounting opposition to GBS. In the face of this opposition, the plaintiffs, with Google's agreement, petitioned the court to delay a hearing that was scheduled for October 17 so that they could rework the settlement. Judge Chin set November 9 as the new deadline when the new version of the settlement would be unveiled.

The great event turned out to be a dud, however. At the last minute, Google and the plaintiffs asked Judge Chin to grant another extension. He gave them four more days, so the witching hour finally took place not on November 9 but on a less auspicious date, Friday the 13th.

Why did the deadline look so monumental? The terms of the settlement will have a profound effect on the book industry for the foreseeable future. On the positive side, Google will make it possible for consumers to purchase access to millions of copyrighted books currently in print and to read them on computer screens or hand-held devices. Many millions more—books covered by copyright but out of print, at least seven million in all, including untold millions of "orphans" whose rightsholders have not been identified—will be available through subscriptions paid for by institutions such as universities. The database, along with books in the public domain that Google has already digitized, will constitute a gigantic digital library, and it will grow over time so that some day it could be larger than the Library of Congress (which now contains over 21 million catalogued books.) By paying a moderate subscription fee, libraries, colleges, and educational institutions of all kinds could have instant access to a whole world of learning and literature.

But will the price be moderate? The negative arguments stress the danger that monopolies tend to charge monopoly prices. Equally important, they warn that Google's dominance of access to books will reinforce its power over access to other kinds of information, raising concerns for privacy (Google may be able to aggregate data about your reading, e-mail, consumption, housing, travel, employment, and many other activities), competition (the class-action character of the suit could make it impossible for another entrepreneur to digitize orphan works, because only Google will be protected from litigation by rightsholders), and commitment to the public good. As a commercial enterprise, Google's first duty is to provide a profit for its shareholders, and the settlement leaves no room for representation of libraries, readers, or the public in general.

An extensive argument about the pros and cons could turn the courtroom in the Southern District of New York into a forum where the full range of literary questions would be dramatized by debate. No courtroom drama took place on November 13, because nothing happened other than the filing of the revised settlement (call it GBS 2.0 to distinguish it from the original version of the settlement, GBS 1.0) But the filing was important in itself because it marked the denouement of years of hard bargaining over who would control a large stretch of the digital landscape that is just now coming in to view.

To be sure, GBS 2.0 will certainly be appealed by groups and individuals who claim they were not fairly represented in the classes of authors and publishers. The case may take years to work its way through the courts. Meanwhile, Google will go on digitizing; and as the legal situation evolves, it may devise further revisions of the settlement (GBS 3.0, GBS 4.0, etc.). The public will have to study all the iterations in order to stay informed about the rules of the game while the game is being played. Who ultimately wins is not simply a matter of competition among potential entrepreneurs but an issue of enormous importance to everyone who cares about books, even though the public is reduced to the role of a spectator.

As the first step toward a resolution, the filing on November 13 suggested just how far Google is willing to go in modifying the original settlement. Google's spokesman hailed the revised version as providing all the benefits and none of the defects that one could expect. According to Dan Clancy, Google Books engineering director,

Google is still very excited about this agreement. . . .We look forward to continuing to work with rightsholders from around the world to fulfill our longstanding mission of increasing access to all the world's books.

But the arguments in favor of the reworked settlement came from Google and the plaintiffs who will become its collaborators if their deal is approved. To get a sense of the counterarguments, one can survey the memorandums and amicus briefs that were filed with the court before November 9.* The protests that came from Europe are the most revealing. Although they concentrate on issues of special importance to foreigners—above all, the incompatibility of American class-action suits with copyright protection for non-Americans—they show how the settlement was seen from a distant perspective.

The governments of France and Germany sent memorandums urging the court to reject the settlement "in its entirety" or at least insofar as it applied to their own citizens. Far from seeing any potential public good in it, they condemned it for creating an "unchecked, concentrated power" over the digitization of a vast amount of literature (this according to the French memorandum) and for doing so (according to the Germans) by a "commercially driven" agreement negotiated "in secrecy . . . behind closed doors by three interested parties: the Authors Guild, the Association of American Publishers and Google, Inc."

In contrast to the commercial character of Google's enterprise, both governments stressed the higher values represented by their national literatures. The French began their

---

*The texts of the documents can be consulted at http://dockets.justia.com/docket/court-nysdce/case_no-1:2005cv08136/case_id-273913.

memorandum by invoking Pascal, Descartes, Molière, Racine, and other writers through Camus and Sartre, while the Germans summoned up the line that led from Goethe and Schiller to Heinrich Böll and Günter Grass. Each country cited the score of its Nobel Prize winners in literature (France 16, Germany 12), and each buttressed its case by other evidence of high-mindedness. The Germans insisted on Gutenberg and his contribution to "the spread of science and culture." The French cited the Declaration of the Rights of Man and of the Citizen from 1789 and the Universal Declaration of Human Rights of 1948 in order to uphold the principle of "free access to information" threatened by Google's "de facto monopoly."

It is an odd spectacle: foreign governments defending a European notion of culture against the capitalistic inroads of an American company and submitting their case to Judge Denny Chin of the Southern District Court of New York. What Judge Chin, who grew up in Hell's Kitchen in a family of poor Chinese immigrants (and won a scholarship to Princeton University) made of it all is difficult to say. He did not tip his hand on November 13, nor did he say when a hearing would take place.

In playing the cultural card, the French emphasized the unique character of the book, "a product unlike other products"—its power to capture creativity, to enrich civilization, and to promote diversity, which, they claimed, would be compromised by Google's commitment to commercialization. The Germans spoke in the name of "the land of poets and thinkers," but they laid most stress on the right of privacy, which, they argued, Google could threaten by keeping data on who reads what. Both governments then listed a series of subsidiary arguments, which were nearly the same, word for word—unsurprisingly, as they engaged the same legal counsel:

1. The settlement gives Google a virtual monopoly over orphan works, even though it has no claim to their copyrights.
2. Its opt-out provision, which means that authors will be deemed to have accepted the settlement unless they notify Google to the contrary, violates the rights inherent in authorship.
3. It contains a most-favored-nation clause—i.e., a provision that prevents a potential competitor from extracting better terms than Google in any new commercial uses of the digitized books. The terms of such future enterprises will be determined by a Book Rights Registry composed exclusively of representatives of the authors and publishers. The Registry will keep track of copyrights and cooperate with Google in setting prices.
4. It gives Google the power to censor its database by excluding up to 15 percent of the digitized works.
5. Its guidelines for pricing will promote Google's commercial interests, not the good of the public, through the use of algorithms created by Google according to Google's secret methods.
6. It favors secrecy in general, hiding audit procedures, preventing the public from attending meetings in which Google and the Registry will discuss library matters, and even requiring Google, the authors, and publishers to destroy all documents relevant to their agreement on the settlement.

Above all, the French and Germans condemned the settlement for sanctioning the "uncontrolled, autocratic concentration of power in a single corporate entity," which threatened the "free exchange of ideas through literature." To drive the point home, they both noted that Google took in more revenue than many countries—$22 billion in 2008.

The same points were made in a hearing before the European Commission on September 7 by the three most important international library associations: the International Federation of Library Associations (IFLA), the European Bureau of Library, Information, and Documentation Associations (EBLIDA), and Ligue des Bibliothèques Européennes de Recherche (LIBER). In nearly identical testimony, all three stressed the danger that "a large proportion of the world's heritage of books in digital format will be under the control of a single corporate entity."

It was Google's sheer power that gave them pause. They summoned up the prospect of a digital library of 30 million books that would cost $750 million dollars, and they concluded that Google would exercise something close to hegemony in the book world. Therefore, they appealed to the European Commission to defend the interests of the public by preventing Google from abusing its power.

Some of these associations submitted similar statements to the New York court. So did hundreds of other groups and individuals. After reading through them, one has the impression of a sense of alarm gathering force and rising to the surface of a collective consciousness. As November 9 approached, it did indeed promise to be a day of destiny, when we would begin to see into our digital future and to face the forces that might determine it.

Where was the Department of Justice in the pre-November debate? It, too, submitted a memorandum for the court's consideration. After months of investigating potential violations of antitrust law, the DOJ pointed to two serious difficulties: the possibility of horizontal agreements among authors and publishers to restrict price competition and the further restriction of competition by Google's de facto exclusive rights to the digital distribution of orphan works. Competitors would be denied access to millions of orphans, the memorandum argued, because they would not enjoy the immunity from suits for copyright infringement that the settlement reserves to Google. Moreover, the settlement's most-favored-nation clause would prevent all competitors from obtaining better terms than Google's even if they could put together an attractive data base. Instead of expatiating in the European manner on the danger to the world's literary heritage, the DOJ warned about something concrete: "the risk of market foreclosure."

What to do? Far from sounding hostile to Google Book Search, the DOJ acknowledged its potential to promote the public good and announced, "The United States does not want the opportunity or momentum to be lost." The memorandum could therefore be read as a prescription for a way to save the settlement. It concentrated on the most hotly debated provisions—those concerning the approximately 7 million out-of-print but in-copyright books, especially orphans—and it suggested the following changes:

1. Require rightsholders of out-of-print books to participate in the settlement by opting in instead of operating from the assumption that they had agreed to participate unless they opted out. The shift to an opt-out default would remove Google's control of books whose rightsholders cannot be identified or do not come forward.

2. Do not distribute the profits from the sale of orphan books to the parties of the settlement (Google and the authors and publishers), but rather use the money to fund a thorough search for the unknown rightsholders and extend the search for a long period of time.

3. Appoint guardians to protect the interests of orphan rightsholders by serving on the Registry.

4. Find some mechanism by which potential competitors to Google could gain access to orphan works without exposure to suits for infringement of copyright. Presumably this would require legislation by Congress.

5. Prevent Google from using out-of-print works in new commercial products without the owner's permission.

The DOJ said it would continue to investigate the potential violation of antitrust laws, and it concluded with an unambiguous imperative: "This Court should reject the Proposed Settlement in its current form. . . ." But its recommendations for an improved settlement did not go far—not nearly as far as those suggested by the governments of France and Germany and many other critics. The DOJ said nothing about the need for monitoring prices, protecting privacy, preventing censorship, providing representation of the public on the Registry, and requiring full disclosure of Google's secret data. If the DOJ encouraged Judge Chin to take a broad view of the settlement, it did not open the door wide.

The revised settlement, or GBS 2.0, released on November 13, reads as if Google and the plaintiffs took most of their cues from the DOJ's memorandum. In a clear concession to the DOJ's criticisms, GBS 2.0 provides that the Registry will include a court-appointed guardian to represent the rightsholders of unclaimed books. But it does not switch to an opt-out default provision for such rightsholders—that is, according to GBS 2.0, any owner of a copyright of an out-of-print book would be deemed to accept the settlement unless he or she rejected it. Because millions of books, primarily orphans, fall into this category where the rightsholders are difficult to identify, Google alone would enjoy immunity from prosecution by any rightsholders who might turn up—and the exposure to litigation, which could easily reach $150,000 per title, would be enough to prevent any competitor from entering the field. Instead of providing a solution to the problem of orphan works, GBS 2.0 leaves Google in command of their commercialization, pending eventual legislation by Congress.

As to revenue from the sale of orphan books, GBS 2.0 complies with the DOJ's insistence that the money not go to Google and the plaintiffs. Instead it will be spent in efforts to search for the unidentified rightsholders; and after being held for ten years, the funds will be distributed to charities determined by court order.

GBS 2.0 also follows the DOJ's recommendation to abandon the most-favored-nation clause. Google's competitors would be able to license out-of-print books in retail enterprises—that is, in selling individual works to consumers—although Google would maintain exclusive control of the institutional subscriptions to its gigantic database.

How the price of those subscriptions will be set remains unclear. GBS 2.0 has some language explaining the way its pricing algorithm will work, but it contains no effective mechanism to prevent price gouging, no provision for an antitrust consent decree that would empower a public authority to monitor prices, and no way to protect the public from excessive pricing should Google be taken over in the future by rapacious speculators.

GBS 2.0 does not therefore differ in essentials from GBS 1.0. It largely ignores the objections of foreign governments, except in one crucial respect: It partly meets the objections by narrowing the scope of GBS to books published in the United States and countries with similar legal systems—that is, the United Kingdom, Canada, and Australia. Google will not display books published in countries like France and Germany, and it will give them representation on the Registry to protect their interests. Just what proportion of unclaimed works will now be excluded from the settlement by this concession remains to be clarified.

Will these concessions be enough to mollify Google's critics outside the Department of Justice who are not parties to the settlement? Probably not, judging from a statement issued on November 13 by the Open Book Alliance, whose members include Microsoft, Amazon, and Yahoo:

> By performing surgical nip and tuck, Google, the AAP [Association of American Publishers], and the AG [Authors Guild] are attempting to distract people from their continued efforts to establish a monopoly over digital content access and distribution; usurp Congress's role in setting copyright policy; lock writers into their unsought Registry, stripping them of their individual contract rights; put library budgets and patron privacy at risk; and establish a dangerous precedent by abusing the class-action process.

What, then, is the outlook for the future? No one can predict the fate of the settlement as it bounces from court to court; but if the public good should be taken into consideration, one can imagine two general solutions to the problems posed by GBS, one maximal, one minimal.

The most ambitious solution would transform Google's digital database into a truly public library. That, of course, would require an act of Congress, one that would make a decisive break with the American habit of determining public issues by private lawsuit. The legislation would have to settle ancillary problems—how to adjust copyright, deal with orphan books, and compensate Google for its investment in digitizing—but it would have the advantage of clearing up a messy legal landscape and of giving the American people what they deserve: a national digital library equal to the needs of the twenty-first century. But it is not clear how Google would react to such a buyout.

If state intervention is deemed to go too far against the American grain, a minimal solution could be devised for the private sector. Congress would have to intervene with legislation to protect the digitization of orphan works from lawsuits, but it would not need to appropriate funds. Instead, funding could come from a coalition of foundations. The digitizing, open-access distribution, and preservation could be done by a non-profit organization such as the Internet Archive, a non-profit group that was built as a digital library of texts, images, and archived Web pages. In order to avoid conflict with interests in the current commercial market, the database would include only books in the public domain and orphan works. Its time span would increase as copyrights expired, and it could include an opt-in provision for rightsholders of books that are in copyright but out of print.

The work need not be done in haste. At the rate of a million books a year, we would have a great library, free and accessible to everyone, within a decade. And the job would be done right, with none of the missing pages, botched images, faulty editions, omitted art work, censoring, and misconceived cataloging that mar Google's enterprise. Bibliographers—who appear to play little or no part in Google's digitizing—would direct operations along with computer engineers. Librarians would cooperate with both in order to assure the preservation of the books, another weak point in GBS because Google is not committed to maintaining its corpus, and digitized texts easily degrade or become inaccessible.

This digitizing process could be subsidized as part of the Obama administration's economic stimulus, and the overall cost, spread out over ten to twenty years, would be manageable, perhaps $750 million in all. Meanwhile, Google and anyone else would be free to exploit the commercial sector. The national digital library could be composed from the holdings of the Library of Congress alone or, failing that, from research libraries that have not opened all their collections to Google.

Perhaps other solutions could be devised. If the court hearing did not resolve the Google Book Search problem on November 13, at least it had the potential to concentrate minds and stimulate public debate. We are agreed that something must be done to improve the nation's health. Why not do something to enrich its culture?

PART I

Future

CHAPTER 1

Google and the Future of Books

FOR THE LAST FOUR YEARS, Google has been digitizing millions of books, including many covered by copyright, from the collections of major research libraries, and making the texts searchable online. This project, known as Google Book Search, triggered a suit by a group of authors and publishers who claimed that Google was violating their copyrights. After lengthy negotiations, the plaintiffs and Google agreed on a settlement, which could have a profound effect on the world of books for the foreseeable future. What will that future be?

No one knows, because the settlement is so complex that it is difficult to perceive the legal and economic contours in the new lay of the land. But those of us who are responsible for research libraries have a clear view of a common goal: we want to open up our collections and make them available to readers everywhere. How to get there? The only workable tactic may be vigilance: see as far ahead as you can; and while you keep your eye on the road, remember to look in the rearview mirror.

When I look backward, I fix my gaze on the eighteenth century, the Enlightenment, its faith in the power of knowledge, and the world of ideas in which it operated—what the enlightened referred to as the Republic of Letters.

The eighteenth century imagined the Republic of Letters as a realm with no police, no boundaries, and no inequalities other than those determined by talent. Anyone could join it by exercising the two main attributes of citizenship, writing and reading. Writers formulated ideas, and readers judged them. Thanks to the power of the printed word, the judgments spread in widening circles, and the strongest arguments won.

The word also spread by written letters, for the eighteenth century was a great era of epistolary exchange. Read through the correspondence of Voltaire, Rousseau, Franklin, and Jefferson—each filling about fifty volumes—and you can watch the Republic of Letters in operation. All four writers debated all the issues of their day in a steady stream of letters, which crisscrossed Europe and America in a transatlantic information network.

I especially enjoy the exchange of letters between Jefferson and Madison. They discussed everything, notably the American Constitution, which Madison was helping to write in Philadelphia while Jefferson was representing the new republic in Paris. They often wrote about books, for Jefferson loved to haunt the bookshops in the capital of the Republic of Letters, and he frequently bought books for his friend. The purchases included Diderot's *Encyclopédie*, which Jefferson thought that he had got at a bargain price, although he had mistaken a reprint for a first edition.

Two future presidents discussing books through the information network of the Enlightenment—it's a stirring sight. But before this picture of the past fogs over with sentiment, I should add that the Republic of Letters was democratic only in principle. In practice, it was dominated by the wellborn and the rich. Far from being able to live from their pens, most writers had to court patrons, solicit sinecures, lobby for appointments to state-controlled journals, dodge censors, and wangle their way into salons and academies, where reputations were made. While suffering indignities at the hands of their social superiors, they turned on one another. The quarrel between Voltaire and Rousseau illustrates their temper. After reading Rousseau's *Discourse on the Origins of Inequality* in 1755, Voltaire wrote to him, "I have received, Monsieur, your new book against the human race. . . . It makes one desire to go down on all fours." Five years later, Rousseau wrote to Voltaire. "Monsieur, . . . I hate you."

The personal conflicts were compounded by social distinctions. Far from functioning like an egalitarian agora, the Republic of Letters suffered from the same disease that ate through all societies in the eighteenth century: privilege. Privileges were not limited to aristocrats. In France, they applied to everything in the world of letters, including printing and the book trade, which were dominated by exclusive guilds, and the books themselves, which could not appear legally without a royal privilege and a censor's approbation, printed in full in their text.

One way to understand this system is to draw on the sociology of knowledge, notably Pierre Bourdieu's notion of literature as a power field composed of contending positions within the rules of a game that itself is subordinate to the

dominating forces of society at large. But one needn't subscribe to Bourdieu's school of sociology in order to acknowledge the connections between literature and power. Seen from
the perspective of the players, the realities of literary life con-
tradicted the lofty ideals of the Enlightenment. Despite its
principles, the Republic of Letters, as it actually operated, was
a closed world, inaccessible to the underprivileged. Yet I want
to invoke the Enlightenment in an argument for openness in
general and for open access in particular.

If we turn from the eighteenth century to the present, do we
see a similar contradiction between principle and practice—
right here in the world of research libraries? One of my colleagues is a quiet, diminutive lady, who might call up the
notion of Marian the Librarian. When she meets people at
parties and identifies herself, they sometimes say conde-
scendingly, "A librarian, how nice. Tell me, what is it like to
be a librarian?" She replies, "Essentially, it is all about money
and power."

We are back with Pierre Bourdieu. Yet most of us would
subscribe to the principles inscribed in prominent places in
our public libraries. "Free to All," it says above the main entrance to the Boston Public Library; and in the words of
Thomas Jefferson, carved in gold letters on the wall of the
Trustees' Room of the New York Public Library: "I look to
the diffusion of light and education as the resource most to
be relied on for ameliorating the condition promoting the
virtue and advancing the happiness of man." We are back
with the Enlightenment.

Our republic was founded on faith in the central principle
of the eighteenth-century Republic of Letters: the diffusion of
light. For Jefferson, enlightenment took place by means of
writers and readers, books and libraries—especially libraries,

at Monticello, the University of Virginia, and the Library of Congress. This faith is embodied in the United States Constitution. Article 1, Section 8, establishes copyright and patents "for limited times" only and subject to the higher purpose of promoting "the progress of science and useful arts." The Founding Fathers acknowledged authors' rights to a fair return on their intellectual labor, but they put public welfare before private profit.

How to calculate the relative importance of those two values? As the authors of the Constitution knew, copyright was created in Great Britain by the Statute of Anne in 1710 for the purpose of curbing the monopolistic practices of the London Stationers' Company and also, as its title proclaimed, "for the encouragement of learning." At that time, Parliament set the length of copyright at fourteen years, renewable only once. The stationers attempted to defend their monopoly of publishing and the book trade by arguing for perpetual copyright in a long series of court cases. But they lost in the definitive ruling of *Donaldson v. Beckett* in 1774.

When the Americans gathered to draft a constitution thirteen years later, they generally favored the view that had predominated in Britain. Twenty-eight years seemed long enough to protect the interests of authors and publishers. Beyond that limit, the interest of the public should prevail. In 1790, the first copyright act—also dedicated to "the encouragement of learning"—followed British practice by adopting a limit of fourteen years renewable for another fourteen.

How long does copyright extend today? According to the Sonny Bono Copyright Term Extension Act of 1998 (also known as the "Mickey Mouse Protection Act," because Mickey was about to fall into the public domain), it lasts as long as the life of the author plus seventy years. In practice, that normally would mean more than a century. Most books published in the twentieth century have not yet entered the public domain. When it comes to digitization, access to our cultural heritage generally ends on January 1, 1923, the date from which great numbers of books are subject to copyright laws. It will remain there—unless private interests take over the digitizing, package it for consumers, tie the packages up by means of legal deals, and sell them for the profit of the shareholders. As things stand now, for example, Sinclair Lewis's *Babbitt*, published in 1922, is in the public domain, whereas Lewis's *Elmer Gantry*, published in 1927, will not enter the public domain until 2022.*

To descend from the high principles of the Founding Fathers to the practices of the cultural industries today is to leave the realm of Enlightenment for the hurly-burly of corporate capitalism. If we turned the sociology of knowledge onto the present—as Bourdieu himself did—we would see

---

*The 1998 Copyright Term Extension Act retroactively lengthened protection by twenty years for books copyrighted after January 1, 1923. Unfortunately, the copyright status of books published in the twentieth century is complicated by legislation that has extended copyright eleven times during the last fifty years. Rightsholders had to renew their copyrights until a 1992 congressional act removed that requirement for books published between 1964 and 1977, when, according to the Copyright Act of 1976, their copyrights would last for the author's life plus fifty years. The 1998 act extended that protection to the author's life plus seventy years. Therefore, all books published after 1963 remain in copyright, and an unknown number—owing to inadequate information about the deaths of authors and the owners of copyright—published between 1923 and 1964 are also protected. See Paul A. David and Jared Rubin, "Restricting Access to Books on the Internet: Some Unanticipated Effects of U.S. Copyright Legislation," *Review of Economic Research on Copyright Issues*, Vol. 5, No. 1 (2008).

that we live in a world designed by Mickey Mouse, red in tooth and claw.

Does this kind of reality check make the principles of Enlightenment look like a historical fantasy? Let's reconsider the history. As the Enlightenment faded in the early nineteenth century, professionalization set in. You can follow the process by comparing the *Encyclopédie* of Diderot, which organized knowledge into an organic whole dominated by the faculty of reason, with its successor from the end of the eighteenth century, the *Encyclopédie méthodique*, which divided knowledge into fields that we can recognize today: chemistry, physics, history, mathematics, and the rest. In the nineteenth century, those fields turned into professions, certified by PhDs and guarded by professional associations. They metamorphosed into departments of universities, and by the twentieth century they had left their mark on campuses—chemistry housed in this building, physics in that one, history here, mathematics there, and at the center of it all, a library, usually designed to look like a temple of learning.

Along the way, professional journals sprouted throughout the fields, subfields, and sub-subfields. The learned societies produced them, and the libraries bought them. This system worked well for about a hundred years. Then commercial publishers discovered that they could make a fortune by selling subscriptions to the journals. Once a university library subscribed, the students and professors came to expect an uninterrupted flow of issues. The price could be ratcheted up without causing cancellations, because the libraries paid for the subscriptions and the professors did not. Best of all, the professors provided free or nearly free labor. They wrote the articles, refereed submissions, and served on editorial boards, partly to spread knowledge in the Enlightenment fashion, but mainly to advance their own careers.

The result stands out on the acquisitions budget of every research library: the *Journal of Comparative Neurology* now costs $25,910 for a year's subscription; *Tetrahedron* costs $17,969 (or $39,739, if bundled with related publications as a *Tetrahedron* package); the average price of a chemistry journal is $3,490; and the ripple effects have damaged intellectual life throughout the world of learning. Owing to the skyrocketing cost of serials, libraries that used to spend 50 percent of their acquisitions budget on monographs now spend 25 percent or less. University presses, which depend on sales to libraries, cannot cover their costs by publishing monographs. And young scholars who depend on publishing to advance their careers are now in danger of perishing.

Fortunately, this picture of the hard facts of life in the world of learning is already going out of date. Biologists, chemists, and physicists no longer live in separate worlds; nor do historians, anthropologists, and literary scholars. The old map of the campus no longer corresponds to the activities of the professors and students. It is being redrawn everywhere, and in many places the interdisciplinary designs are turning into structures. The library remains at the heart of things, but it pumps nutrition throughout the university, and often to the farthest reaches of cyberspace, by means of electronic networks.

The eighteenth-century Republic of Letters had been transformed into a professional Republic of Learning, and it is now open to amateurs—amateurs in the best sense of the word, lovers of learning among the general citizenry. Openness is operating everywhere, thanks to "open access" repositories of digitized articles available free of charge, the Open Content Alliance, the Open Knowledge Commons, OpenCourse-Ware, the Internet Archive, and openly amateur enterprises like Wikipedia. The democratization of knowledge now seems to be at our fingertips. We can make the Enlightenment ideal come to life in reality.

At this point, you may suspect that I have swung from one American genre, the jeremiad, to another, utopian enthusiasm. It might be possible, I suppose, for the two to work together as a dialectic, were it not for the danger of commercialization. When businesses like Google look at libraries, they do not merely see temples of learning. They see potential assets or what they call "content," ready to be mined. Built up over centuries at an enormous expenditure of money and labor, library collections can be digitized en masse at relatively little cost—millions of dollars, certainly, but little compared to the investment that went into them.

Libraries exist to promote a public good: "the encouragement of learning," learning "Free to All." Businesses exist in order to make money for their shareholders—and a good thing, too, for the public good depends on a profitable economy. Yet if we permit the commercialization of the content of our libraries, there is no getting around a fundamental contradiction. To digitize collections and sell the product in ways that fail to guarantee wide access would be to repeat the mistake that was made when publishers exploited the market for scholarly journals, but on a much greater scale, for it would turn the Internet into an instrument for privatizing knowledge that belongs in the public sphere. No invisible hand would intervene to correct the imbalance between the private and the public welfare. Only the public can do that, but who speaks for the public? Not the legislators of the Mickey Mouse Protection Act.

You cannot legislate Enlightenment, but you can set rules of the game to protect the public interest. Libraries represent the public good. They are not businesses, but they must cover their costs. They need a business plan. Think of the old motto of Con Edison when it had to tear up New York's streets in order to get at the infrastructure beneath them: "Dig we must." Libraries say, "Digitize we must." But not on any terms. We must do it in the interest of the public, and that means holding the digitizers responsible to the citizenry.

It would be naive to identify the Internet with the Enlightenment. It has the potential to diffuse knowledge beyond anything imagined by Jefferson; but while it was being constructed, link by hyperlink, commercial interests did not sit idly on the sidelines. They want to control the game, to take it over, to own it. They compete among themselves, of course, but so ferociously that they kill each other off. Their struggle for survival is leading toward an oligopoly; and whoever may win, the victory could mean a defeat for the public good.

Don't get me wrong. I know that businesses must be responsible to shareholders. I believe that authors are entitled to payment for their creative labor and that publishers deserve to make money from the value they add to the texts supplied by authors. I admire the wizardry of hardware, software, search engines, digitization, and algorithmic relevance ranking. I acknowledge the importance of copyright, although I think that Congress got it better in 1790 than in 1998.

But we, too, cannot sit on the sidelines, as if the market forces can be trusted to operate for the public good. We need to get engaged, to mix it up, and to win back the public's rightful domain. When I say "we," I mean we the people, we who created the Constitution and who should make the Enlightenment principles behind it inform the everyday realities of the information society. Yes, we must digitize. But more important, we must democratize. We must open access to our cultural heritage. How? By rewriting the rules of the game, by subordinating private interests to the public good, and by taking inspiration from the early republic in order to create a Digital Republic of Learning.

What provoked these jeremianic-utopian reflections? Google Book Search. Four years ago, Google began digitizing books from research libraries, providing full-text searching and making books in the public domain available on the Internet at no cost to the viewer. For example, it is now possible for anyone, anywhere, to view and download a digital copy of the 1871 first edition of *Middlemarch* that is in the collection of the Bodleian Library at Oxford. Everyone profited, including Google, which collected revenue from some discreet advertising attached to the service. Google also digitized an ever-increasing number of library books that were protected by copyright in order to provide search services that displayed small snippets of the text. In September and October 2005, a group of authors and publishers brought a class-action suit against Google, alleging violation of copyright. On October 28, 2008, after long and secret negotiations, the opposing parties announced agreement on a settlement, which is subject to approval by the US District Court for the Southern District of New York.*

The settlement creates an enterprise known as the Book Rights Registry to represent the interests of the copyright holders. Google will sell access to a gigantic data bank composed

---

*The full text of the settlement can be found at www.googlebooksettlement .com/agreement.html.

primarily of copyrighted, out-of-print books digitized from research libraries. Colleges, universities, and other organizations will be able to subscribe by paying for an "institutional license" providing access to the data bank. A "public access license" will make this material available to public libraries, where Google will provide free viewing of the digitized books on one computer terminal. And individuals also will be able to access and print out digitized versions of the books by purchasing a "consumer license" from Google, which will cooperate with the registry for the distribution of all the revenue to copyright holders. Google will retain 37 percent, and the registry will distribute 63 percent among the rightsholders.

Meanwhile, Google will continue to make books in the public domain available for users to read, download, and print, free of charge. Of the seven million books that Google reportedly had digitized by November 2008, one million are works in the public domain; one million are in copyright and in print; and five million are in copyright but out of print. It is this last category that will furnish the bulk of the books to be made available through the institutional license.

Many of the in-copyright and in-print books will not be available in the data bank unless the copyright owners opt to include them. They will continue to be sold in the normal fashion as printed books and also could be marketed to individual customers as digitized copies, accessible through the consumer license for downloading and reading, perhaps eventually on e-book readers such as the Sony Reader.

After reading the settlement and letting its terms sink in— no easy task, as it runs to 134 pages and 15 appendices of legalese—one is likely to be dumbfounded: here is a proposal that could result in the world's largest library. It would, to be sure, be a digital library, but it could dwarf the Library of

Congress and all the national libraries of Europe. Moreover, in pursuing the terms of the settlement with the authors and publishers, Google could also become the world's largest book business—not a chain of stores but an electronic supply service that could out-Amazon Amazon.

An enterprise on such a scale is bound to elicit reactions of the two kinds that I have been discussing: on the one hand, utopian enthusiasm; on the other, jeremiads about the danger of concentrating power to control access to information.

Who could not be moved by the prospect of bringing virtually all the books from America's greatest research libraries within the reach of all Americans, and perhaps eventually to everyone in the world with access to the Internet? Not only will Google's technological wizardry bring books to readers, it will also open up extraordinary opportunities for research, a whole gamut of possibilities from straightforward word searches to complex text mining. Under certain conditions, the participating libraries will be able to use the digitized copies of their books to create replacements for books that have been damaged or lost. Google will engineer the texts in ways to help readers with disabilities.

Unfortunately, Google's commitment to provide free access to its database on one terminal in every public library is hedged with restrictions: readers will not be able to print out any copyrighted text without paying a fee to the copyright holders (though Google has offered to pay them at the outset); and a single terminal will hardly satisfy the demand in large libraries. But Google's generosity will be a boon to the small-town, Carnegie-library readers, who will have access to more books than are currently available in the New York Public Library. Google can make the Enlightenment dream come true.

But will it? The eighteenth-century philosophers saw monopoly as a main obstacle to the diffusion of knowledge—not merely monopolies in general, which stifled trade according to Adam Smith and the Physiocrats, but specific monopolies such as the Stationers' Company in London and the booksellers' guild in Paris, which choked off free trade in books.

Google is not a guild, and it did not set out to create a monopoly. On the contrary, it has pursued a laudable goal: promoting access to information. But the class-action character of the settlement makes Google invulnerable to competition. Most book authors and publishers who own US copyrights are automatically covered by the settlement. They can opt out of it; but whatever they do, no new digitizing enterprise can get off the ground without winning their assent one by one, a practical impossibility, or without becoming mired down in another class-action suit. If approved by the court—a process that could take as much as two years—the settlement will give Google control over the digitizing of virtually all books covered by copyright in the United States.

This outcome was not anticipated at the outset. Looking back over the course of digitization from the 1990s, we now can see that we missed a great opportunity. Action by Congress and the Library of Congress or a grand alliance of research libraries supported by a coalition of foundations could have done the job at a feasible cost and designed it in a manner that would have put the public interest first. By spreading the cost in various ways—a rental based on the amount of use of a database or a budget line in the National Endowment for the Humanities or the Library of Congress—we could have provided authors and publishers with a legitimate income, while maintaining an open access repository or one in which access was based on reasonable fees. We could have created a National Digital Library—the twenty-first-century equivalent of the Library of Alexandria. It is too late now. Not only have we failed to realize that possibility, but, even worse, we are allowing a question of public policy—the control of access to information—to be determined by private lawsuit.

While the public authorities slept, Google took the initiative. It did not seek to settle its affairs in court. It went about its business, scanning books in libraries; and it scanned them so effectively as to arouse the appetite of others for a share in the potential profits. No one should dispute the claim of authors and publishers to income from rights that properly belong to them; nor should anyone presume to pass quick judgment on the contending parties of the lawsuit. The district court judge will pronounce on the validity of the settlement, but that is primarily a matter of dividing profits, not of promoting the public interest.

As an unintended consequence, Google will enjoy what can only be called a monopoly—a monopoly of a new kind, not of railroads or steel but of access to information. Google has no serious competitors. Microsoft dropped its major program to digitize books several months ago, and other enterprises like the Open Knowledge Commons (formerly the Open Content Alliance) and the Internet Archive are minute and ineffective in comparison with Google. Google alone has the wealth to digitize on a massive scale. And having settled with the authors and publishers, it can exploit its financial power from within a protective legal barrier; for the class action suit covers the entire class of authors and publishers. No new entrepreneurs will be able to digitize books within that fenced-off territory, even if they could afford it, because they would have to fight the copyright battles all over again. If the settlement is upheld by the court, only Google will be protected from copyright liability.

Google's record suggests that it will not abuse its double-barreled fiscal-legal power. But what will happen if its current leaders sell the company or retire? The public will discover the answer from the prices that the future Google charges, especially the price of the institutional subscription licenses. The settlement leaves Google free to negotiate deals with each of its clients, although it announces two guiding principles: "(1) the realization of revenue at market rates for each Book and license on behalf of the Rightsholders and (2) the realization of broad access to the Books by the public, including institutions of higher education."

What will happen if Google favors profitability over access? Nothing, if I read the terms of the settlement correctly. Only the registry, acting for the copyright holders, has the power to force a change in the subscription prices charged by Google, and there is no reason to expect the registry to object if the prices are too high. Google may choose to be generous in its pricing, and I have reason to hope it may do so; but it could also employ a strategy comparable to the one that proved to be so effective in pushing up the price of scholarly journals: first, entice subscribers with low initial rates, and then, once they are hooked, ratchet up the rates as high as the traffic will bear.

Free-market advocates may argue that the market will correct itself. If Google charges too much, customers will cancel their subscriptions, and the price will drop. But there is no direct connection between supply and demand in the mechanism for the institutional licenses envisioned by the settlement. Students, faculty, and patrons of public libraries will not pay for the subscriptions. The payment will come from the libraries; and if the libraries fail to find enough money for the subscription renewals, they may arouse ferocious protests from readers who have become accustomed to Google's service. In the face of the protests, the libraries probably will cut back on other services, including the acquisition of books, just as they did when publishers ratcheted up the price of periodicals.

No one can predict what will happen. We can only read the terms of the settlement and guess about the future. If Google makes available, at a reasonable price, the combined holdings of all the major US libraries, who would not applaud? Would we not prefer a world in which this immense corpus of digitized books is accessible, even at a high price, to one in which it did not exist?

Perhaps, but the settlement creates a fundamental change in the digital world by consolidating power in the hands of one company. Apart from Wikipedia, Google already controls the means of access to information online for most Americans, whether they want to find out about people, goods, places, or almost anything. In addition to the original "Big Google," we have Google Earth, Google Maps, Google Images, Google Labs, Google Finance, Google Arts, Google Food, Google Sports, Google Health, Google Checkout, Google Alerts, and many more Google enterprises on the way. Now Google Book Search promises to create the largest library and the largest book business that have ever existed.

Whether or not I have understood the settlement correctly, its terms are locked together so tightly that they cannot be pried apart. At this point, neither Google, nor the authors, nor the publishers, nor the district court is likely to modify the settlement substantially. Yet this is also a tipping point in the development of what we call the information society. If we get the balance wrong at this moment, private interests may outweigh the public good for the foreseeable future, and the Enlightenment dream may be as elusive as ever.

CHAPTER 2

The Information Landscape

INFORMATION IS EXPLODING so furiously around us and information technology is changing at such bewildering speed that we face a fundamental problem: how to orient ourselves in the new landscape? What, for example, will become of research libraries in the face of technological marvels such as Google? How to make sense of it all? I have no answer to that problem, but I can suggest an approach to it: look at the history of the ways information has been communicated. Simplifying things radically, you could say that there have been four fundamental changes in information technology since humans learned to speak.

Somewhere, around 4000 BC, humans learned to write. Egyptian hieroglyphs go back to about 3200 BC, alphabetical writing to 1000 BC. According to scholars like Jack Goody, the invention of writing was the most important technological breakthrough in the history of humanity. It transformed mankind's relation to the past and opened a way for the emergence of the book as a force in history.

The history of books led to a second technological shift when the codex replaced the scroll sometime soon after the beginning of the Christian era. By the third century AD, the codex—that is, books with pages that you turn as opposed to scrolls that you roll—became crucial to the spread of Christianity. It transformed the experience of reading: the page emerged as a unit of perception, and readers were able to leaf through a clearly articulated text, one that eventually included differentiated words (that is, words separated by spaces), paragraphs, and chapters, along with tables of contents, indexes, and other reader's aids.

The codex, in turn, was transformed by the invention of printing with movable type in the 1450s. To be sure, the Chinese developed movable type around 1045 and the Koreans used metal characters rather than wooden blocks around 1230. But Gutenberg's invention, unlike those of the Far East, spread like wildfire, bringing the book within the reach of ever-widening circles of readers. The technology of printing did not change for nearly four centuries, but the reading public grew larger and larger, thanks to improvements in literacy, education, and access to the printed word. Pamphlets and newspapers, printed by steam-driven presses on paper made from wood pulp rather than rags, extended the process of democratization so that a mass public came into existence during the second half of the nineteenth century.

The fourth great change, electronic communication, took place yesterday, or the day before, depending on how you measure it. The Internet dates from 1974, at least as a term. It developed from ARPANET, which went back to 1969, and from earlier experiments in communication among networks of computers. The Web began as a means of communication among physicists in 1991. Web sites and search engines became common in the mid-1990s. And from that point everyone knows the succession of brand names that have made electronic communication an everyday experience: Gopher, Mosaic, Netscape, Internet Explorer, and Google, founded in 1998.

When strung out in this manner, the pace of change seems breathtaking: from writing to the codex, 4,300 years; from the codex to movable type, 1,150 years; from movable type to the Internet, 524 years; from the Internet to search engines, 17 years; from search engines to Google's algorithmic relevance ranking, 7 years; and who knows what is just around the corner or coming out the pipeline?

Each change in the technology has transformed the information landscape, and the speed-up has continued at such a rate as to seem both unstoppable and incomprehensible. In the long view—what French historians call *la longue durée*—the general picture looks quite clear—or, rather, dizzying. But by aligning the facts in this manner, I have made them lead to an excessively dramatic conclusion. Historians, American as well as French, often play such tricks. By rearranging the evidence, it is possible to arrive at a different picture, one that emphasizes continuity instead of change. The continuity I have in mind has to do with the nature of information itself or, to put it differently, the inherent instability of texts. In place of the long-term view of technological transformations, which underlies the common notion that we have just entered a new era, the information age, I want to argue that every age was an age of information, each in its own way, and that information has always been unstable.

Let's begin with the Internet and work backwards in time. More than a million blogs have emerged during the last few years. They have given rise to a rich lore of anecdotes about the spread of misinformation, some of which sound like urban myths. But I believe the following story is true, though I can't vouch for its accuracy, having picked it up from the Internet myself. As a spoof, a satirical newspaper, *The Onion*, put it out that an architect had created a new kind of building in Washington, D.C., one with a convertible dome. On sunny days, you push a button, the dome rolls back, and it looks like a football stadium. On rainy days it looks like Congress. The story traveled from Web site to Web site until it arrived in China, where it was printed in the *Beijing Evening News*. Then it was taken up by the *Los Angeles Times*, the *San Francisco Chronicle*, Reuters, CNN, Wired.com, and countless blogs as a story about the Chinese view of the United States: they think we live in convertible buildings, just as we drive around in convertible cars.

Other stories about blogging point to the same conclusion: blogs create news, and news can take the form of a textual reality that trumps the reality under our noses. Today many reporters spend more time tracking blogs than they do checking out traditional sources such as the spokespersons of public authorities. News in the information age has broken loose from its conventional moorings, creating possibilities of misinformation on a global scale. We live in a time of unprecedented accessibility to information that is increasingly unreliable. Or do we?

I would argue that news has always been an artifact and that it never corresponded exactly to what actually happened. We take today's front page as a mirror of yesterday's events, but it was made up yesterday evening—literally, by "make-up" editors, who designed page one according to arbitrary conventions: lead story on the far right column, off-lead on the left, soft news inside or below the fold, features set off by special kinds of headlines. Typographical design orients the reader and shapes the meaning of the news. News itself takes the form of narratives composed by professionals according to conventions that they picked up in the course of their training—the "inverted pyramid" mode of exposition, the "color" lead, the code for "high" and "the highest" sources, and so on. News is not what happened but a story about what happened.

Of course, many reporters do their best to be accurate, but they must conform to the conventions of their craft, and there is always slippage between their choice of words and the nature of an event as experienced or perceived by others. Ask anyone involved in a reported happening. They will tell you that they did not recognize themselves or the event in the story that appeared in the paper. Sophisticated readers in the Soviet Union learned to distrust everything that appeared in *Pravda* and even to take non-appearances as a sign of something going on. On August 31, 1980, when Lech Walesa signed the agreement with the Polish government that created Solidarity as an independent trade union, the Polish people refused at first to believe it, not because the news failed to reach them but because it was reported on the state-controlled television.

I used to be a newspaper reporter myself. I got my basic training as a college kid covering police headquarters in Newark in 1959. Although I had worked on school newspapers, I did not know what news was—that is, what events would make a story and what combination of words would make it into print after passing muster with the night city editor. When events reached headquarters, they normally took the form of "squeal sheets" or typed reports of calls received at the central switchboard. Squeal sheets concerned everything from stray dogs to murders, and they accumulated at a rate of a dozen every half hour. My job was to collect them from a lieutenant on the second floor, to go through them for anything that might be news, and to announce the potential news to the veteran reporters from a dozen papers playing poker in the press room on the ground floor. The poker game acted as a filter for the news. One of the reporters would say if something I selected would be worth checking out. I did the checking, usually by phone calls to key offices like the homicide squad. If the information was good enough, I would tell the poker game, whose members would phone it in to their city desks. But it had to be really good—that is, what ordinary people would consider bad—to warrant interrupting the never-ending game. Poker was everyone's main interest—everyone but me: I could not afford to play (cards cost a dollar ante, a lot of money in those days), and I needed to develop a nose for news.

I soon learned to disregard DOAs (dead on arrival, meaning ordinary deaths) and robberies from gas stations, but it took time for me to spot something really "good," like a hold-up in a respectable store or a water main break at a central location. One day I found a squeal sheet that was so good— it combined rape and murder—that I went straight to the homicide squad instead of reporting first to the poker game. When I showed it to the lieutenant on duty, he looked at me in disgust: "Don't you see this, kid?" he said, pointing to a *B* in parentheses after the names of the victim and the suspect. Only then did I notice that every name was followed by a *B* or a *W*. I did not know that crimes involving black people did not qualify as news.

Having learned to write news, I now distrust newspapers as a source of information, and I am often surprised by historians who take them as primary sources for knowing what really happened. I think newspapers should be read for information about how contemporaries construed events, rather than for reliable knowledge of events themselves. A study of news during the American Revolution by a graduate student of mine, Will Slauter, provides an example. Will followed accounts of Washington's defeat at the Battle of Brandywine as it was refracted in the American and European press. In the eighteenth century, news normally took the form of isolated paragraphs rather than "stories" as we know them now, and newspapers lifted most of their paragraphs from each other, adding new material picked up from gossips in coffee houses or ship captains returning from voyages. A loyalist New York newspaper printed the first news of Brandywine with a letter from Washington informing Congress that he had been forced to retreat before the British forces under General William Howe. A copy of the paper traveled by ship, passing from New York to Halifax, Glasgow, and Edinburgh, where the paragraph and the letter were reprinted in a local newspaper.

The Edinburgh reprints were then reprinted in several London papers, each time undergoing subtle changes. The changes were important, because speculators were betting huge sums on the course of the American war, while bears were battling bulls on the Stock Exchange, and the government was about to present a budget to Parliament, where the pro-American opposition was threatening to overthrow the ministry of Lord North. At a distance of 3,000 miles and four to six weeks of travel by ship, events in America were crucial for the resolution of this financial and political crisis.

What had actually happened? Londoners had learned to mistrust their newspapers, which frequently distorted the news as they lifted paragraphs from each other. That the original paragraph came from a loyalist American paper made it suspect to the reading public. Its round-about route made it look even more doubtful, for why would Washington announce his own defeat, while Howe had not yet claimed victory in a dispatch sent directly from Philadelphia, near the scene of the action? Moreover, some reports noted that Lafayette had been wounded in the battle, an impossibility to British readers, who believed (wrongly from earlier, inaccurate reports) that Lafayette was far away from Brandywine, fighting against General John Burgoyne near Canada.

Finally, close readings of Washington's letter revealed stylistic touches that could not have come from the pen of a general. One—the use of "arraying" instead of "arranging" troops—later turned out to be a typographical error. Many Londoners therefore concluded the report was a fraud, designed to promote the interests of the bull speculators and the Tory politicians—all the more so as the press coverage became increasingly inflated through the process of plagiarism. Some London papers claimed that the minor defeat had been a major catastrophe for the Americans, one that had ended with the annihilation of the rebel army and the death of Washington himself. (In fact, he was reported dead four times during the coverage of the war, and the London press declared Benedict Arnold dead 26 times.)

Le Courrier de l'Europe, a French newspaper produced in London, printed a translated digest of the English reports with a note warning that they probably were false. This version of the event passed through a dozen French papers produced in the Low Countries, the Rhineland, Switzerland, and France itself. By the time it arrived in Versailles, the news of Washington's defeat had been completely discounted. The comte de Vergennes, France's foreign minister, therefore continued to favor military intervention on the side of the Americans. And in London, when Howe's report of his victory finally arrived after a long delay (he had unaccountably neglected to write for two weeks), it was eclipsed by the more spectacular news of Burgoyne's defeat at Saratoga. So the defeat at Brandywine turned into a case of miswritten and misread news—a media *non*-event whose meaning was determined by the process of its transmission, like the blogging about the convertible dome and the filtering of crime reports in Newark's police headquarters.

Information has never been stable. That may be a truism, but it bears pondering. It could serve as a corrective to the belief that the speed-up in technological change has catapulted us into a new age, in which information has spun completely out of control. I would argue that the new information technology should force us to rethink the notion of information itself. It should not be understood as if it took the form of hard facts or nuggets of reality ready to be quarried out of newspapers, archives, and libraries, but rather as messages that are constantly being reshaped in the process of transmission. Instead of firmly fixed documents, we must deal with multiple, mutable texts. By studying them skeptically on our computer screens, we can learn how to read our daily newspaper more effectively—and even how to appreciate old books.

Bibliographers came around to this view long before the Internet. Sir Walter Greg developed it at the end of the nineteenth century, and Donald McKenzie perfected it at the end of the twentieth century. Their work provides an answer to the questions raised by bloggers, Googlers, and other enthusiasts of the World Wide Web: Why save more than one copy of a book? Why spend large sums to purchase first editions? Aren't rare book collections doomed to obsolescence now that everything will be available on the Internet? Unbelievers used to dismiss Henry Clay Folger's determination to accumulate copies of the First Folio edition of Shakespeare as the mania of a crank. The First Folio, published in 1623, seven years after Shakespeare's death, contained the earliest collection of his plays, but most collectors assumed that one copy would be enough for any research library. When Folger's collection grew beyond three dozen copies, his friends scoffed at him as Forty Folio Folger. Since then, however, bibliographers have mined that collection for crucial information, not only for editing the plays but also for performing them.

They have demonstrated that 18 of the 36 plays in the First Folio had never before been printed. Four were known earlier only from faulty copies known as "bad" quartos—booklets of individual plays printed during Shakespeare's lifetime, often by unscrupulous publishers using corrupted versions of the texts. Twelve were reprinted in modified form from relatively good quartos; and only two were reprinted without change from earlier quarto editions. Since none of Shakespeare's manuscripts has survived, differences between these texts can be crucial in determining what he wrote. But the First Folio cannot simply be compared with the quartos, because every copy of the Folio is different from every other copy. While being printed in Isaac Jaggard's shop in 1622 and 1623, the book went through three very different issues. Some copies lacked *Troilus and Cressida*, some included a complete *Troilus*, and some had the main text of *Troilus* but without its prologue and with a crossed-out ending to *Romeo and Juliet* on the reverse side of the leaf containing *Troilus*'s first scene.

The differences were compounded by at least 100 stop-press corrections and by the peculiar practices of at least nine compositors who set the copy while also working on other jobs—and occasionally abandoning Shakespeare to an incompetent teenage apprentice. By arguing from the variations in the texts, bibliographers like Charlton Hinman and Peter Blayney have reconstructed the production process and thus arrived at convincing conclusions about the most important works in the English language. This painstaking scholarship could not have been done without Mr. Folger's Folios.

Of course, Shakespeare is a special case. But textual stability never existed in the pre-Internet eras. The most widely diffused edition of Diderot's *Encyclopédie* in eighteenth-century France contained hundreds of pages that did not exist in the original edition. Its editor was a clergyman who padded the text with excerpts from a sermon by his bishop in order to win the bishop's patronage. Voltaire considered the *Encyclopédie* so imperfect that he designed his last great work, *Questions sur l'Encyclopédie*, as a nine-volume sequel to it. In order to spice up his text and to increase its diffusion, he collaborated with pirates behind the back of his own publisher, adding passages to the pirated editions.

In fact, Voltaire toyed with his texts so much that booksellers complained. As soon as they sold one edition of a work, another would appear, featuring additions and corrections by the author. Their customers protested. Some even said that they would not buy an edition of Voltaire's complete works—and there were many, each different from the others—until he died, an event eagerly anticipated by retailers throughout the book trade.

Piracy was so pervasive in early modern Europe that bestsellers could not be blockbusters as they are today. Instead of being produced in huge numbers by one publisher, they were printed simultaneously in many small editions by many publishers, each racing to make the most of a market unconstrained by copyright. Few pirates attempted to produce accurate counterfeits of the original editions. They abridged, expanded, and reworked texts as they pleased, without worrying about the authors' intentions. They behaved as deconstructionists avant la lettre.

The issue of textual stability leads to the general question about the role of research libraries in the age of the Internet. I cannot pretend to offer easy answers, but I would like to put the question in perspective by discussing two views of the library, which I would describe as grand illusions—grand and partly true.

To students in the 1950s, libraries looked like citadels of learning. Knowledge came packaged between hard covers, and a great library seemed to contain all of it. To climb the steps of the New York Public Library, past the stone lions guarding its entrance and into the monumental reading room on the third floor, was to enter a world that included everything known. The knowledge came ordered into standard categories which could be pursued through a card catalogue and into the pages of the books. In colleges everywhere the library stood at the center of the campus. It was the most important building, a temple set off by classical columns, where one read in silence: no noise, no food, no disturbances beyond a furtive glance at a potential date bent over a book in quiet contemplation.

Students today still respect their libraries, but reading rooms are nearly empty on some campuses. In order to entice the students back, some librarians offer them armchairs for lounging and chatting, even drinks and snacks, never mind about the crumbs. Modern or postmodern students do most of their research at computers in their rooms. To them, knowledge comes online, not in libraries. They know that libraries could never contain it all within their walls, because information is endless, extending everywhere on the Internet, and to find it one needs a search engine, not a card catalogue. But this, too, may be a grand illusion—or, to put it positively, there is something to be said for both visions, the library as a citadel and the Internet as open space. We have come to the problems posed by Google Book Search.

In 2006 Google signed agreements with five great research libraries—the New York Public, Harvard, Michigan, Stanford, and Oxford's Bodleian—to digitize their books. Books in copyright posed a problem, which soon was compounded by lawsuits from publishers and authors. But putting that aside, the Google proposal seemed to offer a way to make all book learning available to all people, or at least those privileged enough to have access to the World Wide Web. It promised to be the ultimate stage in the democratization of knowledge set in motion by the invention of writing, the codex, movable type, and the Internet.

Now, I speak as a Google enthusiast, although I worry about its monopolistic tendencies. I believe Google Book Search really will make book learning accessible on a new, worldwide scale, despite the great digital divide that separates the poor from the computerized. It also will open up possibilities for research involving vast quantities of data, which could never be mastered without digitization. As an example of what the future holds, I would cite the Electronic Enlightenment, a project sponsored by the Voltaire Foundation of Oxford. By digitizing the correspondence of Voltaire, Rousseau, Franklin, and Jefferson—about 200 volumes in superb, scholarly editions—it will, in effect, re-create the trans-Atlantic republic of letters from the eighteenth century. The letters of many other philosophers, from Locke and Bayle to Bentham and Bernardin de Saint-Pierre, will be integrated into this data base, so that scholars will be able to trace references to individuals, books, and ideas throughout the entire network of correspondence that undergirded the Enlightenment. Many such projects—notably American Memory sponsored by the Library of Congress,* and The Valley of the Shadow created at the University of Virginia**—have demonstrated the feasibility and usefulness of data bases on this scale. But their success does not prove that Google Book Search, the largest undertaking of them all, will make research libraries obsolete. On the contrary, Google will make them more important than ever. To support this view, I would like to organize my argument around eight points.

According to the most utopian claim of the Googlers, Google can put virtually all printed books online.

That claim is misleading, and it raises the danger of creating false consciousness, because it may lull us into neglecting our libraries. What percentage of the books in the United States—never mind the rest of the world—will be digitized by Google: 75%? 50%? 25%? Even if the figure is 90%, the residual, non-digitized books could be important. I recently discovered an extraordinary libertine novel, *Les Bohémiens*, by an unknown author, the marquis de Pelleport, who wrote

---

*It is, according to the site, "a digital record of American history and creativity," including sound recordings, prints, maps, and many images.

**An archive of letters, diaries, official records, periodicals, and images documenting the life of two communities—one Northern, one Southern—200 miles apart in the Shenandoah Valley during the years 1859–1870.

it in the Bastille at the same time that the marquis de Sade was writing his novels in a nearby cell. I think that Pelleport's book, published in 1790, is far better than anything Sade produced; and whatever its esthetic merits, it reveals a great deal about the condition of writers in pre-Revolutionary France. Yet only six copies of it exist, as far as I can tell, none of them available on the Internet.* (The Library of Congress, which has a copy, has not opened its holdings to Google.)

If Google missed this book, and other books like it, the researcher who relied on Google would never be able to locate works of great importance. The criteria of importance change from generation to generation, so we cannot know what will matter to our descendants. They may learn a lot from studying our harlequin novels or computer manuals or telephone books. Literary scholars and historians today depend heavily on research in almanacs, chapbooks, and other kinds of "popular" literature, yet few of those works from the seventeenth and eighteenth centuries have survived. They were printed on cheap paper, sold in flimsy covers, read to pieces, and ignored by collectors and librarians who did not consider them as "literature." A researcher in Trinity College, Dublin, recently discovered a drawer full of forgotten ballad books, each one the only copy in existence, each priceless in the eyes of the modern scholar, though it had seemed worthless two centuries ago.

Although Google pursued an intelligent strategy by signing up five great libraries, their combined holdings will not come close to exhausting the stock of books in the United States.

---

*See my article, "Finding a Lost Prince of Bohemia," *New York Review of Books*, April 3, 2008, pp. 44–48.

Contrary to what one might expect, there is little redundancy in the holdings of the five libraries: 60 percent of the books being digitized by Google exist in only one of them. There are about 543 million volumes in the research libraries of the United States. Google reportedly set its initial goal of digitizing at 15 million. As Google signs up more libraries—at last count, 31 American libraries are participating in Google Book Search—the representativeness of its digitized data base will improve. But it has not yet ventured into special collections, where the rarest works are to be found. And of course the totality of world literature—all the books in all the languages of the world—lies far beyond Google's capacity to digitize.

Although it is to be hoped that the publishers, authors, and Google will settle their dispute, it is difficult to see how copyright will cease to pose a problem.

According to the copyright law of 1976 and the copyright extension law of 1998, most books published after 1923 are currently covered by copyright, and copyright now extends to the life of the author plus seventy years. For books in the public domain, Google will allow readers to view the full text and print every page. For books under copyright, however, Google will display only part of the text. Google may persuade the publishers and authors to surrender their claims to books published between 1923 and the recent past, but will it get them to modify their copyrights in the present and future? In 2006, 291,920 new titles were published in the United States, and the number of new books in print has increased nearly every year for the last decade, despite the spread of electronic publishing. How can Google keep up with current production while at the same time digitizing all the books accumulated over the centuries? Better to increase the acquisitions of our research libraries than to trust Google to preserve future books for the benefit of future generations. Google defines its mission as the communication of information—right now, today; it does not commit itself to conserving texts indefinitely.

Companies decline rapidly in the fast-changing environment of electronic technology.

Google may disappear or be eclipsed by an even greater technology, which could make its data base as outdated and inaccessible as many of our old floppy disks and CD-ROMs. Electronic enterprises come and go. Research libraries last for centuries. Better to fortify them than to declare them obsolete, because obsolescence is built into the electronic media.

Google will make mistakes.

Despite its concern for quality and quality control, it will miss books, skip pages, blur images, and fail in many ways to reproduce texts perfectly. Once we believed that microfilm would solve the problem of preserving texts. Now we know better.

As in the case of microfilm, there is no guarantee that Google's copies will last.

Bits become degraded over time. Documents may get lost in cyberspace, owing to the obsolescence of the medium in which they are encoded. Hardware and software become extinct at a distressing rate. Unless the vexatious problem of digital preservation is solved, all texts "born digital" belong to an endangered species. The obsession with developing new media has inhibited efforts to preserve the old. We have lost 80 percent of all silent films and 50 percent of all films made before World War II. Nothing preserves texts better than ink imbedded in paper, especially paper manufactured before the nineteenth century, except texts written in parchment or engraved in stone. The best preservation system ever invented was the old-fashioned, pre-modern book.

Google plans to digitize many versions of each book, taking whatever it gets as the copies appear, assembly-line fashion, from the shelves; but will it make all of them available?

If so, which one will it put at the top of its search list? Ordinary readers could get lost while searching among thousands of different editions of Shakespeare's plays, so they will depend on the editions that Google makes most easily accessible. Will Google determine its relevance ranking of books in the same way that it ranks references to everything else, from toothpaste to movie stars? It now has a secret algorithm to rank Web pages according to the frequency of use among the pages linked to them, and presumably it will come up with some such algorithm in order to rank the demand for books. But nothing suggests that it will take account of the standards prescribed by bibliographers, such as the first edition to appear in print or the edition that corresponds most closely to the expressed intention of the author. Google employs thousands of engineers but, as far as I know, not a single bibliographer. Its innocence of any visible concern for bibliography is particularly regrettable in that most texts, as I have just argued, were unstable throughout most of the history of printing. No single copy of an eighteenth-century best-seller will do justice to the endless variety of editions. Serious scholars will have to study and compare many editions, in the original versions, not in the digitized reproductions that Google will sort out according to criteria that probably will have nothing to do with bibliographical scholarship.

Even if the digitized image on the computer screen is accurate, it will fail to capture crucial aspects of a book.

For example, size. The experience of reading a small duodecimo, designed to be held easily in one hand, differs considerably from that of reading a heavy folio propped up on a book stand. It is important to get the feel of a book— the texture of its paper, the quality of its printing, the nature of its binding. Its physical aspects provide clues about its existence as an element in a social and economic system; and if it contains margin notes, it can reveal a great deal about its place in the intellectual life of its readers.

Books also give off special smells. According to a recent survey of French students, 43 percent consider smell to be one of the most important qualities of printed books—so important that they resist buying odorless electronic books. CaféScribe, a French online publisher, is trying to counteract that reaction by giving its customers a sticker that will give off a fusty, bookish smell when it is attached to their computers.

When I read an old book, I hold its pages up to the light and often find among the fibers of the paper little circles made by drops from the hand of the vatman as he made the sheet— or bits of shirts and petticoats that failed to be ground up adequately during the preparation of the pulp. I once found a fingerprint of a pressman enclosed in the binding of an eighteenth-century *Encyclopédie*—testimony to tricks in the trade of printers, who sometimes spread too much ink on the type in order to make it easier to get an impression by pulling the bar of the press.

I realize, however, that considerations of "feel" and "smell" may seem to undercut my argument. Most readers care about the text, not the physical medium in which it is embedded; and by indulging my fascination with print and paper, I may expose myself to accusations of romanticizing or of reacting like an old-fashioned, ultra-bookish scholar who wants nothing more than to retreat into a rare book room. I plead guilty. I love rare book rooms, even the kind that make you put on gloves before handling their treasures. Rare book rooms are a vital part of research libraries, the part that is most inaccessible to Google. But libraries also provide places for ordinary readers to immerse themselves in books, quiet places in comfortable settings, where the codex can be appreciated in all its individuality.

In fact, the strongest argument for the old-fashioned book is its effectiveness for ordinary readers. Thanks to Google, scholars are able to search, navigate, harvest, mine, deep link, and crawl (the terms vary along with the technology) through millions of Web sites and electronic texts. At the same time, anyone in search of a good read can pick up a printed volume and thumb through it at ease, enjoying the magic of words as ink on paper. No computer screen gives satisfaction like the printed page. But the Internet delivers data that can be transformed into a classical codex. It already has made print on demand a thriving industry, and it promises to make books available from computers that will operate like ATM machines: log in, order electronically, and out comes a printed and bound volume. Perhaps some day a text on a hand-held screen will please the eye as thoroughly as a page of a codex produced two thousand years ago.

Meanwhile, I say: shore up the library. Stock it with printed matter. Reinforce its reading rooms. But don't think of it as a warehouse or a museum. While dispensing books, most research libraries operate as nerve centers for transmitting electronic impulses. They acquire data sets, maintain digital repositories, provide access to e-journals, and orchestrate information systems that reach deep into laboratories as well as studies. Many of them are sharing their intellectual wealth with the rest of the world by permitting Google to digitize their printed collections. Therefore, I also say: long live Google, but don't count on it living long enough to replace that venerable building with the Corinthian columns. As a citadel of learning and as a platform for adventure on the Internet, the research library still deserves to stand at the center of the campus, preserving the past and accumulating energy for the future.

CHAPTER 3

The Future of Libraries

WHAT IS THE FUTURE of research libraries, and how can we prepare for it? These questions cannot be dismissed as "academic"—the kind professors knock about without any consequences for the general citizenry—because they go to the heart of what every citizen seeks every day: information and help in sorting through information for pertinent knowledge.

When I try to foresee the future, I look into the past. Here, for example, is a futuristic fantasy published in 1771 by Louis Sébastien Mercier in his best-selling utopian tract, *The Year 2440*. Mercier falls asleep and wakes up in the Paris that will exist seven centuries after his birth in 1740. He finds himself in a society purged of all the evils from the ancien régime. In the climactic chapter of volume one, he visits the national library, expecting to see thousands of volumes splendidly arrayed as in the Bibliothèque du roi under Louis XV. To his astonishment, however, he finds only a modest room with four small bookcases. What happened to the enormous quantity of printed matter that had accumulated since the eighteenth century, when it had already become unmanageable? he asks. We burned it, the librarian replies: 50,000 dictionaries, 100,000 works of poetry, 800,000 volumes of law, 1.6 million travel books, and 1 billion novels. A commission of virtuous scholars read through it all, eliminated the falsehoods, and boiled it down to its essence: a few basic truths and moral precepts, which fit easily into the four bookcases.

Mercier was a militant advocate of enlightenment and a true believer in the printed word as an agent of progress. He did not favor book burning. But his fantasy expressed a sentiment that was already strong in the eighteenth century and has now become an obsession—the sense of being overwhelmed by information and of helplessness before the need to find relevant material amidst a mountain of ephemera.

One solution to this double problem could be a library without books. In place of Mercier's residual bookcases, it would contain computer terminals, which would provide access to gigantic databases, and readers would find what they wanted by means of search engines tuned to perfection by the latest algorithms.

Sound far-fetched? It is already being built, although it does not call itself a library. It is called Google Book Search. By digitizing the holdings from dozens of research libraries, Google is creating a database composed of millions of books, so many millions that soon it will have constructed a digital mega-library greater than anything ever imagined, except in the fiction of Jorge Luis Borges.

What distinguishes Google's library from others is not digitization in itself, for that exists everywhere, but rather the scale of the scanning and its purpose. Google is a commercial enterprise whose primary goal is to make money. Libraries exist to supply books to readers—books and other materials, some of them digitized. The underlying commercial mission of Google emerged in full view on October 28, 2008, when it announced that it had reached a settlement with a group of authors and publishers who were suing it for alleged breach of copyright. The settlement created a complex mechanism for sharing the income that will be generated by selling access to Google's database. Its most important provision from the perspective of research libraries is an institutional subscription. By paying an annual fee to Google, the libraries will make it possible for their readers to tap all the information in the books that Google has digitized, except for books that are covered by copyright and whose copyright owners have chosen not to make them available through the institutional subscription.

The bargain looked dubious to some of us in charge of the libraries. We had provided Google with the books free of charge in the first place, and now we were being asked to buy back access to them, along with those of our sister libraries, in digitized form. More important, we worried that Google was creating a monopoly, a monopoly of a new kind, potentially greater than any that had previously existed, a monopoly of access to information.

The people at Google find the m-word objectionable. To spare their sensitivity, one could speak of a hegemonic, financially unbeatable, technologically unassailable, and legally invulnerable enterprise that can crush all competition. But in plain English, Google Book Search is a monopoly.

It is a monopoly for three reasons. First, de facto: after Microsoft abandoned the field, no competitor had the technological and financial power to stand up to Google. Second, because of the class-action character of the suit, the settlement covers all authors and publishers in the class of rightsholders. Therefore, a rival to Google would have to win the agreement of every owner of a copyright and settle innumerable suits for copyright infringement at rates that would range from $30,000 to more than $100,000. (At the same time, the settlement would make Google and the plaintiffs the effective owners of books whose copyrights have not been claimed—a complex issue, involving millions of works and not merely the so-called orphan books.) Third, the settlement contains a most-favored-nation clause, which prevents any competitor from receiving better terms than those accorded to Google.

Monopolies are not necessarily bad. In the case of communication by telephone service and travel by railroad, a single company might provide better service than a profusion of baby Bells and New Jersey Transit–type railways. Google could bring its magnificent digital library within the range of readers in public libraries and small colleges everywhere in the country, perhaps someday everywhere in the world.

But do we want one commercial enterprise to have exclusive control of so much information? Libraries are already worried about turning their patrons' records over to the government as could be required by the Patriot Act. Google could know more about us than the CIA, the FBI, and the IRS combined. It could know what we read, what we buy, whom we visit, how many square feet we have in our bedroom, what messages we exchange with our correspondents, and if it gets its algorithms right, what we are likely to think when faced with a decision.

Not that there is anything satanic about Google's ambitions or insincere about its slogan, "Do no evil." The growth of Google's power will merely result from the success of its business plan. Like any business, its first obligation is to produce a profit for its shareholders, not to worry about the public welfare. It may seem that the public has nothing to fear from a monopoly of access to information, because information exists everywhere. We are drowning in it. But consider the power inherent in Google's gatekeeping function. Anyone who commands the portals to digital data can act as a toll collector, making you pay to enter the information highway. In the case of books, the digital copies in Google's database will belong to Google, and Google can charge any price it likes for access to them. It will own a vast stretch of the road.

The settlement includes some vague guidelines for setting prices, but it contains no provision for preventing them from skyrocketing. Google will have to agree on price levels with the Book Rights Registry, which will handle copyright claims and disburse payments. But the registry will be run by representatives of the authors and publishers, who will have an interest in ratcheting up the prices. The party with the greatest interest of all is the public, yet the public has no voice in the settlement. Libraries, schools, universities, ordinary citizens, everyone who reads books but does not belong to the class of copyright owners—all are excluded from the courtroom deliberations that will determine the settlement's fate.

If the judge adheres to standard practices in class-action suits, he may limit his role to verifying that the settlement treats the interests of the contending parties fairly. If he takes a broad view of the issues, he could refuse to authorize the settlement and direct the parties to come back with an improved version. The improvements could include: (1) regular monitoring of prices by a public authority, (2) representation of libraries and readers on the registry, (3) a provision for unclaimed works to be made available for digitization by potential competitors to Google, (4) a requirement that Google seek an antitrust consent decree from the Department of Justice to prevent it from abusing its monopolistic power, and (5) some measure to protect the privacy of individuals from Google's all-seeing electronic eye.

One could imagine an even happier ending: legislation that would make all of Google's data publicly available. Any citizen could consult it, and any company could exploit it. The copyright laws would have to be rewritten, the rightsholders compensated, and Google indemnified for its investment in scanning. It could keep its secret algorithms and continue its search service, but its data bank would become public property. We would have a national digital library.

That dream may be as impossible as Mercier's utopia. To bring the discussion down to a more realistic level, it would be best to assume that some version of Google Book Search will survive as a private enterprise. What then will be the role of research libraries in the new digital environment? They exist in many varieties: the Library of Congress, in a class by itself; state university libraries, some with collections of amazing richness; and a profusion of nongovernment institutions—the Morgan in New York, the Newberry in Chicago, the Huntington in Los Angeles, and the libraries of private universities scattered across the country. What sets apart the American as opposed to the European library system is its variety, especially in the private sector. Even the New York Public Library is private, despite its name and the state subsidies that support its many branches. There is strength in diversity and health in independence from government control. But some private libraries may seem objectionable in one respect: their exclusiveness.

The greatest libraries belong to the most exclusive universities, such as Harvard, Yale, Princeton, and Stanford. Although they admit researchers from the outside world, they remain closed to the public. Some members of the public might object that they turn their backs to the general citizenry and reserve their riches for the privileged few.

I occasionally entertained such thoughts when I enjoyed the privilege of being a graduate student at Oxford. In my day, the Oxford colleges were shut off from outsiders by high walls topped with spikes and jagged glass. The gates of my own college, St. John's, slammed shut at ten o'clock in the evening. If you were outside after ten, you could ring a bell and pay a fine or try to scale the wall—a daunting experience, unless you were tipped off by a fellow student who knew of some clandestine passage by way of a lamppost and a low-hanging roof, a gap in the spikes, or some other chink in the fortifications—which the dean of students left unguarded, according to an implicit contract allowing boys to be boys. (Except for a few female establishments, the colleges were then exclusively male.)

The barriers to outsiders combined with the insider knowledge about how to break the rules reinforced a general sense of exclusiveness. If the architecture were not enough to get across the message, you could read about it in Thomas Hardy's *Jude the Obscure*, which describes Jude's attempts to penetrate the world of learning behind Oxford's forbidding walls. I haven't reread the novel in years, but as I remember it from discussions in St. John's, Jude never made contact with the life inside the colleges, and one of his sons succumbed to the curse on the outsider by murdering the other children and then hanging himself in a room of the Lamb and Flag, a pub located just outside a spot in the wall of the college where I used to climb in.

Harvard's neo-Georgian houses hardly lend themselves to that kind of melodrama, but they can appear forbidding to outsiders. The library offers a way for Harvard to open itself to the public, not physically (the number of readers would make that impossible) but digitally, by sharing its intellectual wealth through the Internet. Openness is the guiding principle that we will pursue in order to adapt the library to the conditions of the twenty-first century. With apologies for their parochialism but in hope that these remarks may be useful to others, I would like to describe some of the measures we have taken.

———

Following the vote of several Harvard faculties in favor of open access, the library has established an Office for Scholarly Communication (OSC), which administers a repository for storing and making available online and free of charge all scholarly articles produced within a participating faculty, except those that the authors choose to exclude. The OSC also plans to digitize dissertations and make them accessible from the same repository, unless their authors prefer to keep them in "dark storage" for a limited time by taking advantage of a similar opt-out provision. While funneling finished scholarship to the outside world, the OSC also will collect "gray" literature—special lectures, conference proceedings, laboratory notes, data sets, reports on work in progress—in a way that will make the intellectual life of the university accessible to anyone who wants to tune in. Of course, there are plenty of problems to be faced: copyright clearance, quality controls, compatibility of systems for searching and storing the data, and the need for funds to build and maintain a digital infrastructure. But at Harvard as at many other universities, the library is strategically placed to act as a nerve center for collecting and diffusing knowledge.

The library is expanding this function through its Open Collections Program. Supported by grants from the Hewlett and Arcadia foundations, it has digitized books, pamphlets, manuscripts, prints, and photographs scattered through dozens of its libraries that have a common connection to specific subjects: Women Working, 1800–1930; Immigration to the United States, 1789–1930; Contagion: Historical Views of Diseases and Epidemics; Expeditions and Discoveries: Sponsored Exploration and Scientific Discovery in the Modern Age; and Islamic Heritage. Teams of professors, librarians, museum curators, and technologists select, catalog, digitize, and make the material available free of charge from Web sites. Each project takes about eighteen months to produce, and each brings a huge number of documents within the reach of students as well as advanced researchers. The material has been translated into seventy-two languages and consulted by hundreds of thousands of visitors around the world.

Outreach to the rest of the world is a responsibility that weighs heavily on Harvard, because the university library contains so much material that does not exist elsewhere. Archives that go back to the founding of the College in 1636 reveal a great deal about the origins of education in America—and of America itself. Special collections scattered through the library system also contain much of importance to other countries. Harvard's Yenching Library has more than 200 unique copies of Chinese works. They, too, will be digitized along with 51,542 rare volumes in a cooperative, open-access project to be conducted with the National Library of China from 2010 to 2016. Harvard hopes to digitize its Ukrainian material, the greatest collection in the world—and one of vital importance to the Ukrainian people, who lost most of their literary heritage during the tragedies that overwhelmed their country during the twentieth century. Harvard's enormous collections in zoology, botany, and medicine are also being digitized and made available through open-access outlets such as the Biodiversity Heritage Library and the journals of the Public Library of Science. Digitization on this scale requires collaboration among several institutions. Many research libraries house special collections that remain unprocessed and unknown, except to a few specialists. Only by making them available through collective action and open access can we fulfill our obligation to the world of learning.

We also must assume another responsibility: the collecting and preserving of material "born digital." Web sites have proliferated across the Internet. Having grown up helter-skelter as the result of individual enterprise, they tend to be resistant to search engines, mutually incompatible in the design of their metadata, and ephemeral: they disappear easily into cyberspace. We have developed a Web Archive Collection Service (WAX) for collecting and preserving this kind of material, and three pilot projects have demonstrated the feasibility of doing so on a large scale: the Edwin O. Reischauer Institute has systematically collected discussions of political issues from more than one hundred Japanese Web sites, and this material is now being stored and preserved in a digital database known as "Constitutional Revision in Japan." The Arthur and Elizabeth Schlesinger Library has developed a similar collection, "Capturing Women's Voices," which will preserve the record of postings by women in relatively obscure blogs. And the Harvard University Archives has launched a program to preserve the records of daily business conducted from the vast number of Web sites that have grown up within Harvard itself. We are also experimenting with plans to archive the millions of messages exchanged within the university by e-mail.

The e-mail problem exists everywhere, of course, and it involves so many complexities, legal as well as technological, that it may be insoluble. Because so much business is transacted over the World Wide Web, we are losing the record of most contemporary communication. Admittedly, the Committee on the Records of Government exaggerated the threat when it proclaimed in 1985 that "the United States is in danger of losing its memory," and the notorious "loss" of the 1960 census is actually a myth. By elaborate and expensive engineering, the Census Bureau recovered most of the data that, in 1976, appeared to be irretrievable, owing to obsolescent hardware. But most government agencies used e-mail by the mid-1980s, and most of that correspondence has been lost—not all of the six million e-mail messages produced each year by the Clinton White House, but apparently even more e-mail from the Bush administration between 2001 and 2005 and more still from the record of business conducted at lower levels of government. We are nibbling at the edges of the problem, but we have not found a solution. Harvard maintains a large information technology section within its library, and its technologists have led the way toward interim solutions through a program known as the Library Digital Initiative. Nonetheless, the problem remains, and it is compounded by difficulties in raising money, developing business plans, and working out general strategies.

The financial constraints are forcing us to rethink our old ways of doing business and to look for reinforcement among potential allies who face similar problems. One natural alliance could link university libraries with university presses.

They rarely have anything to do with each other, even when they are neighbors on the same campus, yet they exist for the same purpose: to spread knowledge. Perhaps we suffer from too narrow a notion of publication, something we associate exclusively with professionals who produce journals and books. To publish means "to make public," a general activity, which was understood in a broad manner from the fourteenth century onward, according to the Oxford English Dictionary: "to make generally accessible or available for acceptance or use."

That definition has a strange resemblance to Google's mission statement: "to organize the world's information and make it universally accessible and useful." Should we think of Google as a publisher? Research libraries certainly fit the broad definition. They "make accessible" all sorts of information, whether as articles deposited in repositories, digitized dissertations, electronic data sets, Web sites, videotaped lectures, conference proceedings, films—or, for that matter, books. Several university libraries—MIT, Stanford, Pennsylvania State—have absorbed their university presses. We have no such plans at Harvard, where the university press continues to thrive, despite the hard times. But we are cooperating with the Press in exploring possibilities for online publishing. One possibility is open-access monographs, available for free online and for purchase in hard copy through print on demand. Another might involve the expertise at the Press for managing peer review and designing digital publications that do not fit into conventional categories such as "monograph" and "article"—for example, annotated editions of collections, proceedings of conferences, and databases.

Most authors today produce electronic texts, and most publishers maintain their backlists in digital repositories. A world in which books are "born digital" and readers are "digital natives" is a world in which research libraries will no longer need to stock huge amounts of current literature in printed form. Print on demand and improved electronic readers will be sufficient to satisfy immediate needs. To be sure, that world still seems far away, and we cannot reduce our acquisitions of printed monographs until we have solved a great many problems, above all the problem of preserving digital texts.

When and if that future is assured, research libraries will be able to concentrate on what has always been their strength: special collections. Those collections in the future may involve materials of a kind that we cannot imagine today. But they will be richer than ever in their holdings of old-fashioned books and manuscripts. Having hoarded their treasures for centuries, libraries will at last be able to share them with the rest of the world. Google will have scanned nearly everything in standard collections, but it will not have penetrated deeply into rare book rooms and archives, where the most important discoveries are to be made. By digitizing their special collections and making them available on open access, research libraries will have realized a crucial aspect of their mission.

But I may be letting my fondness for books of the past distort my vision of the future. No matter how advanced the technology, I cannot imagine that a digitized image of an old book will provide anything comparable to the excitement of contact with the original. When I was a freshman at Harvard in 1957, I discovered that undergraduates were allowed in Houghton Library (Harvard's library for rare books and manuscripts). Summoning up my courage, I walked in and asked if, as I had heard, they possessed Melville's copy of

Emerson's *Essays*. It appeared on my desk in a matter of minutes. Because Melville had written extensive notes in the margins, I found myself reading Emerson through Melville's eyes—or at least attempting to do so.

One bit of marginalia has remained fixed in my memory. It had to do with Melville's experience of rounding Cape Horn in what must be the roughest water in the world. At that time I thought the world in general was pretty rough, so I was primed to sympathize with a caustic note next to a passage about stormy weather. Emerson had been expatiating on the world soul and the transient nature of suffering, which, as any sailor could testify, would blow over like a storm. Melville wondered in the margin whether Emerson had any idea of the terror faced by sailors on whaling ships at the Horn. I read it as a lesson about the Pollyannaish side of Emerson's philosophy.

Back in Harvard a half century later, the memory suddenly surfaced, accompanied by a question: had I got it right? Never mind about all the appointments on the calendar. I hotfooted it to Houghton again.

The opportunity to experiment with déjà vu does not come often. Here is the result, a passage on page 216 of "Prudence" in *Essays: by R. W. Emerson* (Boston, 1847), which Melville marked in pencil in the outer margin with a big *X*: "The terrors of the storm are chiefly confined to the parlour and the cabin. The drover, the sailor, buffets it all day, and his health renews itself at as vigorous a pulse under the sleet, as under the sun of June." At the bottom of the page, Melville scribbled another *X* and wrote: "To one who has weathered Cape Horn as a common sailor, what stuff all this is."

The marginal remark was even sharper than I had recollected, and the sensation of holding Melville's Emerson, a small volume in a cheap cloth binding, in my own hands was even more moving. That kind of experience can only be had in rare book rooms. Yet a digitized image of page 216 of "Prudence" would be enough to help anyone read Emerson through Melville. In fact, digitization can make it possible to see things that are invisible to the unaided eye, as scholars have learned by manipulating digital versions of texts like the oldest manuscript of *Beowulf*.

Of course, the current situation calls for more than hit-or-miss initiatives in digitizing special collections. If research libraries are to flourish in the future, they must band together. They prospered in the twentieth century by pursuing self-interest independently of one another and of interference by the state. But in the twenty-first century, they face the impossible task of advancing on two fronts, the analog and the digital. Their acquisitions budgets cannot bear the weight. Therefore, they must form coalitions, agreeing to invest in some subjects while leaving others to their allies. They must develop common off-site depositories, perfect interlibrary loans, exchange documents electronically, prepare interoperative metadata, integrate their catalogs, and coordinate their digitizing.

Experiments of this kind have been tried and failed, I know. But we must try again. Through trial and error, we must inch forward toward the creation of a national and then an international digital library. Google has demonstrated its feasibility and also the danger of getting it wrong—that is, of favoring private profit at the expense of the public good.

Technological changes wash over the information landscape too rapidly for anyone to know what it will look like ten years from now. But now is the time to act, if we want to channel change for the benefit of everyone. We need action by the state to prevent monopoly and interaction among the libraries to promote a common program. Digitize and democratize—not an easy formula, but the only one that will do if we really mean to realize the ideal of a republic of letters, which once seemed hopelessly utopian.

CHAPTER 4

Lost and Found in Cyberspace

This and the following essay were written in March 1999, when I was launching the Gutenberg-e program at the American Historical Association and at the same time designing an e-book that I planned to write myself. Ten years later, I am still writing it, but I have completed nearly all the documentation, which I soon will make accessible from a Web site while continuing to draft the main body of the text.

LIKE MANY ACADEMICS, I am about to take the leap into cyberspace, and I'm scared. What will I find out there? What will I lose? Will I get lost myself?

As I approach the edge of the Web, I am seized with affection for the media of yesteryear: the lecture and the book. Is it not remarkable that both are still going strong on our campuses, after centuries of use, despite the advent of the so-called Information Age?

Much as I admire my younger colleagues, who splice computerized music and images into their lectures, I find it best to talk right at my students armed with nothing more than chalk and a blackboard. I'm a historian; and when I work in the archives, I fill index cards with notes and sort them into shoe boxes, while all around me the younger generation taps away at portable PCs and uploads images of documents on digital cameras. I love books, old-fashioned books, the older the better. As I see it, book culture reached its highest peak when Gutenberg modernized the codex; and the codex is superior in some ways to the computer. You can leaf through it, annotate it, take it to bed, and store it conveniently on a shelf.

Aside from their mechanical defects, computerized texts communicate a specious sense of mastery over space and time. They have links to the Web, and we think of the Web as infinite. We believe that it connects us with everything, because everything is digitized, or soon will be. Given a powerful enough search engine, we imagine that we can have access to knowledge about anything on earth—and anything from the past. It is all out there on the Internet, waiting to be downloaded and printed out.

Such a notion of cyberspace has a strange resemblance to Saint Augustine's conception of the mind of God—omniscient and infinite, because His knowledge extends everywhere, even beyond time and space. Knowledge could also be infinite in a communication system where hyperlinks extended to everything—except, of course, that no such system could possibly exist. We produce far more information than we can digitize, and information isn't knowledge, anyhow. To know the past, we must dig up its remains and learn how to make sense of them. Most people are content to leave the spade work to historians and to make their own sense from the books those scholars write.

Unfortunately, books, too, have their limits. Any author knows how much must be eliminated before a text is ready for printing, and any researcher knows how little can be studied in the archives before the text is written. The manuscripts seem to stretch into infinity. You open a box, take out a folder, open the folder, take out a letter, read the letter, and wonder what connects it with all the other letters in all the other folders in all the boxes, not just in this repository but in all the archives everywhere. The overwhelming majority have never been read by researchers. And most people never wrote letters. Most human beings have vanished into the past without leaving a trace of their existence. To write history from the archives is to piece together what little we can grasp in as meaningful a picture as we can compose. But the result, in the form of a history book, can no more capture the infinity of experience than Augustine could comprehend the mind of God.

In short, the traditional media have no greater claim than the electronic media to mastery of the past. But there is something unreal about these speculations. The vision of databases or manuscript boxes stretching out to infinity provides no comfort to historians chasing themes through archives. Whatever their epistemological angst, they have concrete problems to solve. In my case, I have dozens of shoe boxes filled with index cards crying out to be transformed into a book—too many, in fact, to squeeze into a single book, too many even to get under control. That is why I contemplate the leap: I want to write an electronic book.

Here is how my fantasy takes shape. An "e-book," unlike a printed codex, can contain many layers arranged in the shape of a pyramid. Readers can download the text and skim through

the topmost layer, which will be written like an ordinary monograph. If it satisfies them, they can print it out, bind it (binding machines can now be attached to computers and printers),
and study it at their convenience in the form of a custom-made
paperback. If they come upon something that especially interests them, they can click down a layer to a supplementary essay
or appendix. They can continue deeper through the book,
through bodies of documents, bibliography, historiography,
iconography, background music, everything I can provide to
give the fullest possible understanding of my subject. In the end,
they will make the subject theirs, because they will find their
own paths through it, reading horizontally, vertically, or diag-
onally, wherever the electronic links may lead.

I realize that describing an e-book is one thing, creating it
another. But the temptation to try is difficult to resist for anyone who has had the archival experience that I just described.
Once I managed to read my way through all the boxes of an
archive, the papers of a French-Swiss publisher, the Société typographique de Neuchâtel: 50,000 letters, the only complete
archive of a publishing house from the eighteenth century that
has survived. I also read most of the documents in two of the
largest collections at the Bibliothèque Nationale de France:
the Collection Anisson-Duperron and the papers of the
Chambre syndicale de la Communauté des libraires et des imprimeurs de Paris. Taken together, these documents give an
amazingly rich view of the world of books in the age of Enlightenment, but it took me eleven summers and three win-
ters over a period of twenty-five years to read them.

Not that I suffered. Neuchâtel is a lovely city in good wine
country on the edge of a lake behind a handsome range of
mountains, and Paris is paradise. The research yielded several
books and articles. But it left me with thousands of index

cards that I have never used—and also with a feeling that I had not got across the full richness of my subject. The documents reveal not only what publishers printed but how they decided what to publish; not only where the books went but how they were handled by smugglers and wagoners at each stage along the transportation systems; not only who wrote them but how the writers understood the enterprise of writing; not only what the king decreed to control the book trade but how censors, police inspectors, bureaucrats, and spies collaborated in the work of repression. The material opens up new ways of thinking about the history of ideas, economics, politics, and society. It raises the possibility of realizing the ideal that the French call *histoire totale*—a total history of the book as a force in France on the eve of the Revolution.

Easier said than done. In earlier efforts to do it, I drafted a 100-page chapter about paper as an ingredient of books and left it in a drawer. I produced 75 pages on the book trade in the Loire Valley and found it so loaded down with detail that no one would want to read it. I prepared a study of how a smuggler in Lyon opened a passage to the rich book country of the Rhône delta, another of how a bookseller in Besançon mounted an ingenious scheme to get around the *ordonnance* against piracy in 1777, another on the *entrepôt* trade in Versailles, another about the life of a literary agent in Paris, another on the adventures of a sales rep (he spent five months flogging books from horseback through most of southern and central France; the horse gave out in Loudun, where he bought a used nag, all of the transactions detailed in his expense account). . . . I could go on and on, listing one promising subject after another; but I could not fit them into a book. There was too much to tell. Whenever I started a new chapter, I found myself pursuing so much detail that the stories ran away with me; and I had to stop, undone by the fear of spending the rest of my life as the chronicler of the Société typographique de Neuchâtel and of writing tomes that no one would read, even if someone might publish them.

The answer is an e-book. Not that an electronic publication offers shortcuts, nor that I intend to dump everything from my shoe boxes onto the Internet. Instead, I plan to work through the material in different ways, covering the most essential topics in the topmost narrative and including mini-monographs along with selections from the richest runs of documents in the lower layers. My readers will be able to help themselves to as much as they like in the portions they prefer and even to link my work with that of others in the burgeoning field of book history. An electronic book about the history of books in the age of Enlightenment! I can't resist. I'll take the leap.

Whatever becomes of my story, I hope it may be useful for others in similar situations. No two situations are truly similar, I know. Few historians have enjoyed the luxury of working for decades in virgin archives. But everyone with a PhD has experienced the difficulties of imposing readable form on intractable matter. I am convinced that the Internet will transform the world of learning. The transformation has already begun. Our task, I think, is to take charge of it so that we maintain the highest standards from the past while developing new ones for the future. What better place to begin than with students now completing dissertations? Having spent their childhood with computers, they will know where they are going when they leap into cyberspace. I still stand on its edge, clutching my shoe boxes and whatever intellectual baggage that may keep me afloat, including some very ancient books, like Augustine's *Confessions* and *The City of God*.

PART II

Present

CHAPTER 5

E-Books and Old Books

When it originally appeared in the New York Review of Books *on March 18, 1999, this essay contained a detailed account of inflation in the prices of scholarly journals and of the disastrous effects of the excessive prices on libraries, university presses, and the careers of young scholars. Those conditions still exist. In fact, they have become worse than ever, but I have condensed the discussion of them here because the same theme appears in some of the following essays, and I want to avoid repeating myself.*

MARSHALL MCLUHAN'S FUTURE has not happened. The Web, yes; global immersion in television, certainly; media and messages everywhere, of course. But the electronic age did not drive the printed word into extinction, as McLuhan prophesied in 1962. His vision of a new mental universe held together by post-printing technology now looks dated. If it fired imaginations for decades in the twentieth century, it does not provide a map for the millennium that we are now entering. The "Gutenberg galaxy" still exists, and "typographic man" is still reading his way around it.

Consider the book. It has extraordinary staying power. Ever since the invention of the codex sometime close to the birth of Christ, it has proven to be a marvelous machine— great for packaging information, convenient to thumb through, comfortable to curl up with, superb for storage, and remarkably resistant to damage. It does not need to be upgraded or downloaded, accessed or booted, plugged into circuits or extracted from webs. Its design makes it a delight to the eye. Its shape makes it a pleasure to hold in the hand. And its handiness has made it the basic tool of learning for thousands of years, even when it had to be unrolled to be read (in the form of the volumen or scroll rather than the codex, composed of leaves connected to a binding) long before Alexander the Great founded the library of Alexandria in 332 BC.

Why then do we continue to hear prophecies about the death of the book? Not because McLuhan was right but because movable type can't move fast enough to keep up with events. Most "e-books" store texts after downloading them from online booksellers and then project them onto a screen, one page at a time. JSTOR, a project developed by The Andrew W. Mellon Foundation, has made vast runs of scholarly periodicals available online and purchasable by libraries who could not afford the originals. The New York Public Library dispenses so much information electronically to readers all over the world that already in 1999 it reported ten million hits on its computer system each month as opposed to 50,000 books checked out in its reading room at 42nd Street. Everything, it seems, is being digitized, and every digit hyperlinked to all the others. If the future brings newspapers without paper, journals without pages, and libraries without walls, what will become of the traditional book? Will electronic publishing wipe it out?

We have heard that prophecy repeated ever since the first e-book, a clunking monstrosity known as Memex, was designed in 1945. By now, the conventional book has been pronounced dead so often that many of us have stopped worrying about the threat of empty shelves. Now that they have computers, Americans produce and consume more paper with print on it than ever. Even Bill Gates, chairman of Microsoft, confessed in a recent speech that he prefers printed paper to computer screens for extensive reading:

> Reading off the screen is still vastly inferior to reading off of paper. Even I, who have these expensive screens and fancy myself as a pioneer of this Web Lifestyle, when it comes to something over about four or five pages, I print it out and I like to have it to carry around with me and annotate. And it's quite a hurdle for technology to achieve to match that level of usability.

Gates says that technology will have to improve "very radically" before "all the things we work with on paper today move over into digital form." In short, the old-fashioned codex, printed on folded and gathered sheets of paper, is not about to disappear into cyberspace.

Why then the continuing fascination with electronic publishing? It seems to have passed through three stages: an initial phase of utopian enthusiasm, a period of disillusionment, and a new tendency toward pragmatism. At first we thought we could create an electronic space, throw everything into it, and leave the readers to sort it out. Then we learned that no one would read a book on a computer screen or wrestle through heaps of printouts. Now we face the possibility of supplementing the traditional book with electronic publications specifically designed for certain purposes and publics.

The best case to be made for e-books concerns scholarly publishing, not in all fields but in large stretches of the humanities and social sciences where conventional monographs have become prohibitively expensive to produce. The difficulty is so severe, in fact, that it is transforming the landscape of learning. It results from three problems that have converged in a way that makes the monograph look like an endangered species.

Commercial publishers have raised the price of periodicals, especially in the natural sciences, to such a height that they have created havoc in the budgets of research libraries. In order to maintain their collections of periodicals, libraries have cut back drastically in their purchases of monographs. Faced with the decline in orders from libraries, university presses have virtually ceased publishing in the least fertile fields. And scholars in those fields no longer have an adequate outlet for their research. The crisis concerns the operation of the market place, not the value of the scholarship; and it is greatest among those with the greatest need to overcome it— the next generation of academics whose careers depend upon their ability to break into print.

A closer look at each aspect of the crisis indicates that it began in the 1970s, when prices of periodicals began to spiral upward. Now they have spun out of control. By 2007, the subscription price for many scientific journals came to more than $20,000 a year. *Nuclear Physics A & B*, for example, cost $21,003, and the expenditures on serials among research libraries had increased by 320 percent over the last two decades. The prestige of publication in the most expensive journals is so important for career advancement, especially in the hard sciences, that university libraries find it impossible to persuade faculty members to accept the cancellation of subscriptions. Therefore, they cope with the pressure on their budgets by sacrificing monographs to periodicals. Until recently, monographs used to account for at least half their acquisitions budgets. Now it often amounts to 25 percent.

The second aspect of the crisis threatens academic life at a particularly vulnerable point: the budgets of university presses. According to a rule of thumb among editors in the 1970s, a university press could count on selling 800 copies of a monograph to libraries. Today the figure is close to 300 and not enough to cover costs. Publishers can no longer be sure of selling books that would have been irresistible to librarians twenty years ago. Volume 1 of *The Papers of Benjamin Franklin*, published in 1959, sold 8,047 copies. Volume 33, published in 1997, sold 753 copies. University presses have often responded to the drop in scholarly demand by publishing fewer scholarly books. Instead, they concentrate on books about popular local themes or birds or cookery or sports or "midlist" books—that is, the quasi-trade works that commercial publishers were neglecting in order to speculate on books with mass appeal: exercise books, how-to books, and potential best-sellers by name-brand authors. Some may object that we have too many monographs—more and more about less and less, as the saying goes. Critics sometimes accuse professors of writing for each other instead of treating subjects that interest the general citizenry. Certainly, monographism can be a disease. It seems to be killing disciplines like literary criticism, where voguishness and arcane jargon have alienated ordinary readers. But most scholars have resisted the most malignant varieties of the disease, and some kinds of scholarship are important but unavoidably esoteric. The question remains: can an author with a worthwhile monograph—something solid but not sexy, the kind of book that flourished twenty years ago—expect to get it published?

If you ask professors and publishers, you are bound to be discouraged. Many of them can tell tales about excellent monographs that did not sell. My own favorite horror story concerns a superb work on the French Revolution that won three major prizes and sold 183 copies in cloth, 549 in paper. Of course some fields, such as the American Civil War, continue to hold up well. No field can be written off, although presses have abandoned several of them and the very notion of a distinct field seems problematic in many disciplines. The scholarly landscape remains too complex to be divided neatly into sectors; but if taken as a whole and looked at as a market, it appears depressed. Whether or not whole presses will go under, one conclusion seems clear: the monograph is indeed endangered.

The danger spills over into the third problem area: the careers of young scholars. Any assistant professor knows the categorical imperative, publish or perish, which translates into something more immediate: no monograph, no tenure. It is difficult enough for a recent PhD to get a job, but that is when the greatest difficulties begin—moving to a new location, getting up courses for the first time, finding a partner or founding a family, and, on top of it all, publishing a book. Suppose against all odds an assistant professor succeeds in transforming a dissertation into a first-rate monograph within three or four years, will he or she be able to get it published? Not likely.

Walk into the office of any editor in a university press, and you will see dissertations stacked in piles, dozens of them. The editor will explain with a sigh that the press can afford to publish only two or three a year, adding with a deeper sigh that the press comes under pressure from tenure committees, who want to see a book in print, accompanied by readers' reports and reviews.

Presses resist being drawn into the tenuring process, and rightly so, but often for the wrong reasons—that is, because they pay more attention to the bottom line of their budgets than to the dividing line of professional responsibilities. Like it or not, they function as a funnel in the process of professional advancement, yet they cannot publish most of the manuscripts they receive. The authors of those manuscripts probably will not make it to the next stage of their careers. Instead, they may fall into the floating population of adjunct teachers, picking up odd jobs wherever they can find them, usually for inadequate pay, insufficient benefits, and no recognition. We may be producing the intellectual equivalent of the Okies and Arkies from the dust-bowl years—migrant academic workers with laptop computers who live out of the backseats of their cars.

Given these intersecting, overlapping problems, can electronic publishing provide a solution? Phase one of the infatuation with e-books, the period of utopian enthusiasm, stands as a warning against unrealistic expectations. The utopians have a blind faith in the effectiveness of the Invisible Hand so dear to economists. Let the entrepreneurs slug it out on the market place, they say, and the good search engines will drive out the bad e-messages.

This argument may be valid for some kinds of consumer goods, perhaps even for the consumption of trade books, considering the success of enterprises like Amazon.com. But for those who worry about scholarship, and intellectual life in general, the argument smacks of Micawberism: do nothing, and something might turn up. In fact, cyberspace, like the economy, needs to be regulated. Scholars should set standards. They should maintain quality control in the academic world, and they can do so by attacking the crisis at two points: the point where beginners turn dissertations into books and the point where veterans experiment with new kinds of scholarship.

Certainly, we can dump unlimited numbers of dissertations onto the Web. Several programs exist for providing this service—and it is a genuine service: it makes research available to readers. But as a rule, this kind of publication provides only information, not fully developed scholarship, at least not in most of the humanities and social sciences. Anyone who has read raw dissertations knows what I mean: dissertations are not books. A world of difference separates them. To become a book, a dissertation must be reorganized, trimmed here and expanded there, adapted to the needs of a lay reader, and rewritten from top to bottom, preferably under the guidance of an experienced editor.

Editors often refer to this reworking as "value added," and they add only some of the value that goes into a book. Peer review, page design, composition, printing, marketing, publicity—a whole array of expertise is necessary to transform a dissertation into a monograph. Instead of simplifying this process, electronic publishing will add further complications, but the result could be a great increase in value. An e-dissertation could contain unlimited appendices and databases. It could be linked to other publications in a manner that would permit readers to find new paths through old material. And once the technical problems are worked out, it could be produced and distributed economically, saving production costs for the publisher and shelf space for the library.

Of course, the problems are enormous. Start-up costs are high; and prices won't be low, at least not until individual presses can offer whole collections of e-monographs and libraries can buy them in quantity, making them accessible to readers through site licenses. The readers will download them, search the texts for whatever needs to be studied, print out the relevant sections, bind them in a machine attached to the printer, and take them home for reading in the form of a custom-made paperback. The technology already exists to perform all these functions. In fact, paperback versions of existing books can be produced electronically for much less than $50. But in order to publish original, high-quality monographs, a university press will have to put together all the parts of an original, high-quality system for production and distribution.

In the case of history, a discipline where the crisis in scholarly publishing is particularly acute, the attraction of an e-book should be especially appealing. Any historian who has done long stints of research knows the frustration over his or her inability to communicate the fathomlessness of the archives and the bottomlessness of the past. If only my reader could have a look inside this box, you say to yourself, at all the letters in it, not just the lines from the letter I am quoting. If only I could follow that trail in my text just as I pursued it through the dossiers, when I felt free to take detours leading away from my main subject. If only I could show how themes criss-cross outside my narrative and extend far beyond the boundaries of my book. Not that books should be exempt from the imperative of trimming a narrative down to its sheerest shape. But instead of using an argument to close a case, they could open up new ways of making sense of the evidence, new possibilities of apprehending the raw material embedded in the story, a new consciousness of the complexities involved in construing the past.

I am not advocating the sheer accumulation of data, nor arguing for links to data banks. So-called hyperlinks can merely be an elaborate form of footnoting. Instead of bloating the book, I think it possible to structure it in layers arranged like a pyramid. The top layer could be a concise account of the subject, available perhaps in paperback. The next layer could contain expanded versions of different aspects of the argument, not arranged sequentially as in a narrative, but rather as self-contained units that feed into the topmost storey. The third layer could be composed of documentation, possibly of different kinds, each set off by interpretive essays. A fourth layer might be theoretical or historiographical, with selections from previous scholarship and discussions of them. A fifth layer could be pedagogic, consisting of suggestions for classroom discussion, a model syllabus, and course packets. And a sixth layer could contain readers' reports, exchanges between the author and the editor, and letters from readers, who could provide a growing corpus of commentary as the book made its way through different publics.

A new book of this kind would elicit a new kind of reading. Some readers might be satisfied with a quick run through the upper narrative. Others might want to read vertically, pursuing certain themes deeper and deeper into the supporting essays and documentation. Still others might navigate in unanticipated directions, seeking connections that suit their own interests or reworking the material into constructions of their own. In each case, the appropriate texts could be printed and bound according to the specifications of the reader. The computer screen would be used for sampling and searching, whereas concentrated, long-term reading would take place by means of the conventional codex.

Far from being utopian, the electronic monograph could meet the needs of the scholarly community at the points where its problems converge. It could provide a tool for prying problems apart and opening up a new space for the extension of knowledge. The world of learning is changing so rapidly that no one can predict what it will look like ten years from now. But I believe it will remain within the Gutenberg galaxy—though the galaxy will expand, thanks to a new source of energy, the electronic book, which will act as a supplement to, not a substitute for, Gutenberg's great machine.

CHAPTER 6

Gutenberg-e

BY 1997 SO MANY problems had converged in the world of books that fundamental change seemed possible. I hoped to do something about them, at least in a small way, because I thought I could involve the American Historical Association in a project to promote a new kind of monograph: PhD dissertations reworked for publication online as electronic books. Having been elected to become president of the AHA in 1999, I devoted most of 1997–98 to planning the project, which came to be known as Gutenberg-e.

First I prepared a preliminary sketch in the hope of finding funding. Its main purpose, as I originally envisaged it and still understand it in retrospect, was to develop and test a model for publishing scholarly books through the Internet. It also had two other aims: to revitalize the monograph in fields of history where conventional publishing had proved to be uneconomical and to help beginning scholars launch careers, despite the difficulties of breaking into print in the conventional manner.

Having now studied dozens of profit-and-loss statements, I can see that my understanding of the economics of publishing was, at best, naïve. I imagined at first that the e-books could be made available online free of charge—in effect, as open-access publications to be subsidized by foundations or universities, who would cover costs long enough to see whether the experiment was a success. When I sounded the Andrew W. Mellon foundation about this possibility in February 1998, I received an encouraging reply with a disconcerting query attached to it: What was my business plan? I had never heard of a business plan. True, I had picked up some knowledge about the economics of publishing when I served on the Editorial Board of the Princeton University Press from 1977 through 1981. But I did not understand my lack of understanding. As a rank amateur, I believed that e-books offered a way to save costs, not on the editorial side, where expertise would remain as crucial as ever, but in paper, printing, and binding, and in expenditure on warehousing, transportation, handling at the retail level, and shelving in libraries.

Moreover, it seemed likely that e-books would attract buyers, especially in research libraries, because they would open up the possibility of communicating research in a new manner. Thanks to digitization, their authors could provide limitless documentary evidence, illustrations, sound recordings, film, and links to other publications, making it all accessible in combinations that would go far beyond the capacity of the printed codex. Of course, the history profession was notorious for its conservatism in professional matters. But if we could find a way to select the very best dissertations and to work them up in model publications, their sheer quality might win over the skeptics. The success of the e-books in history would set standards for all sorts of scholarly publishing online; and by breaking through the barriers that had dammed up publishing in print, it would clear a way for new academic careers.

The difficulty of getting published in fields like colonial Latin America and early modern Europe made the curse of publish-or-perish weigh heavily on the younger generation of scholars. To be sure, they faced demographic, economic, and many other disadvantages in the struggle to win tenure. But the moment when a new PhD faced the necessity of converting his or her dissertation into a book seemed to be the point at which the most urgent problems came together. If we could focus our efforts on that critical juncture, we might be able to develop a new mode of disseminating knowledge, legitimize scholarly e-books, and promote academic careers, all at the same time.

I developed these arguments in the first sketch of the project, which I submitted to the Mellon Foundation early in 1998. Then as now, the leaders of Mellon were eager to support experiments that held promise for improving basic conditions in the world of learning. I had developed friendly relations with them from an earlier experiment, "The East-West Seminar in Eighteenth-Century Studies," which brought together young scholars from both sides of the Iron Curtain for a week of intense debate about questions that cut across academic as well as political divisions. That project, which I directed for seven years thanks to funding from Mellon, may have won me a sympathetic hearing for the e-book enterprise. In any case and whatever the cause may have been, the people at Mellon responded favorably to my request for support and awarded me a preliminary grant to cover the costs of convening a committee of experts, who were to investigate

different aspects of the plan and come up with recommendations for a final grant proposal.

Composed for the most part of savvy publishers and librarians, the committee exposed the amateurism behind my
ideas when it met on October 10, 1998. Sanford Thatcher,
Director of the Penn State Press, warned that it was impossible to determine distinct fields in which the monograph could
be considered a clearly "endangered species." In fact, one
committee member remarked, "I find myself hard-pressed to
say which fields are 'endangered' when the whole enterprise
seems to be in trouble." Colin Day, then Director of the University of Michigan Press, insisted that preparing an electronic
publication would involve more, not fewer, costs, owing to
technical complexities and the imperatives of design: how
would the editors and engineers construct a work that would
have the "look and feel" required for success in promoting a
new mode of communication? And Ann Okerson, associate
university librarian at Yale, exposed the potential incompatibility of the three objectives I had outlined. Was it really
possible to kill three birds with one stone? she asked.
Nonetheless, the committee endorsed the general idea of developing model e-monographs in order to prepare a way for
scholarly publishing in a future that everyone agreed was
certain to be digital. I submitted a more modest proposal in
late October, and Mellon awarded the AHA a generous
grant to create a series of electronic history books known as
Gutenberg-e.

From 2000 to 2006, the AHA sponsored an annual competition for the best history dissertations, which were chosen
by juries of distinguished senior historians. The rationale for
the program, as the original proposal had explained (the final
proposal used more formal language) was "to sanction elec-

tronic publishing by showering the winners with so much honor that tenure committees and academic administrations would sit up and take notice. If successful, the example could spread and help change the rules of the game in academic life. It could also promote scholarly communication of a new kind at a time when publishers and librarians are perplexed about how to take the first steps in the difficult and dangerous field of electronic publishing." The winners, normally six a year, received prizes of $20,000 each, which they were expected to spend on additional research and whatever expenses were necessary to rework their dissertations as electronic books.

They needed help, of course. As a publisher, we chose the most helpful press that we could find, Columbia University Press, which was already committed to electronic publishing, thanks to the success of CIAO (Columbia International Affairs Online), its collection of articles and working papers on international relations available online by subscription. While the AHA organized the prize competitions, Kate Wittenberg directed the publication of Gutenberg-e from Columbia. She organized biannual workshops, supported by a further grant from Mellon, in which the newly chosen prize winners discussed their projects as a group and then conferred privately with editors, computer engineers, designers, and other book professionals. Prize winners from previous years attended the workshops, as did editors from other houses. The experience gained at Columbia therefore began to spread through the publishing industry as well as the university world.

Before the workshops could produce results, however, we ran into unanticipated difficulties. There were surprisingly few applicants, despite a great deal of publicity and press coverage, during the first years of the competition. We learned that dissertation supervisors discouraged their students from competing, because they feared that an online publication would not count as a true book when it came to hiring and tenure decisions. Inflexible notions of what constituted a book also prevented the first Gutenberg-e monographs from getting widely reviewed. Michael Grossberg, the editor of the *American Historical Review*, helped overcome this obstacle by developing a protocol for reviewing e-books in general, and Columbia sent out printed copies of the electronic texts to reviewers who did not want to click around on computer screens. In order to increase the number of applicants, we opened the competition to a broader range of subjects and finally gave up altogether in our attempt to revive the monograph in fields deemed to be endangered.

Thanks to these efforts and intense publicity by the AHA, both in its newsletter, *Perspectives*, and at the award ceremonies in its annual meeting, applications picked up during the last years of the program. By then, however, we had to confront another problem: although the prize-winning dissertations were superb and the prize winners represented the finest talent of their generation, few of the authors could complete their e-books on schedule. Writing a book, as opposed to a dissertation, took more time than they had imagined, and writing an electronic book turned out to be doubly difficult. They ran into problems of clearing rights and purchasing illustrative material. Many of them started families, moved to new jobs, and stayed up late writing lectures or feeding babies. How could they find time or energy to compose an ambitious, new kind of book?

As a consequence of these difficulties, Columbia's production pipeline became clogged, and the delayed output hurt sales, which generally took place through site licenses purchased by libraries. The annual subscription, for access to all the books as a digital package, cost $195. Individual e-books sold for $49.50. By January 2005, when the program came to an end, enough institutional subscriptions had been sold, according to Kate Wittenberg's calculations, to cover costs. At that time, however, Columbia, like many university presses, had come under severe economic pressure. It decided that it could not finance a trimmed-down version of the program—the AHA was willing to continue its administration of the competition but the prizes would have to be honorific—after the lapse of the Mellon subsidy in 2005. In the end, Columbia made the entire corpus, 35 works, available on an open-access platform. At the same time, the books were assimilated into a parallel program developed by the American Council of Learned Societies, Humanities E-Book, where they are available by subscription and will be preserved indefinitely.

Can Gutenberg-e be considered a success? I think it fair to say that, taken individually, the books represented the highest quality and the most innovative scholarship from the graduate students who entered the profession in the first decade of the twenty-first century. Some, like *The Door of the Seas and Key to the Universe: Indian Politics and the Imperial Rivalry in the Darien, 1640–1750* by Ignacio Gallup-Diaz, do not differ greatly in their "look and feel" from printed monographs, because they are designed to be read linearly, page by page and chapter after chapter. Others, such as *Binding Memories: Women as Makers and Tellers of History in Magude, Mozambique* by Heidi Gengenbach, employ audio, video, images, and hyperlinked texts in ways that invite the reader to jump around in many directions, following search functions and links. Taken as a whole, the e-books explored a broad range of the possibilities created by digital technology.

Reviews were generally favorable but not enthusiastic. No reviewer disputed the excellence of the scholarship, and none stinted in praising the individual volumes. But the series as a whole looked disappointing to Patrick Manning, a professor at Northeastern University, who published the most thorough critique of it. "The Gutenberg-e books make solid contributions to their fields but do not now appear as breakthroughs, either as individual works or as a group,"* he concluded. Sanford Thatcher, who followed the project at a critical distance from its beginning, wrote a more positive assessment at its end: "We are still a long way from finding a solution to creating a viable transition for monographs from print to electronic environments. . . . But the Gutenberg-e project . . . should remain as a source of inspiration and experiential knowledge for many years to come and will undoubtedly prove to have been well worth the investment in the long run."**

It should be possible sometime in the not too distant future to reach a consensus about the value of Gutenberg-e, because experimentation in electronic publishing hardly compares with world-historical phenomena that defy conclusive interpretations—the kind evoked by Mao Tse-tung in his famous (and probably apocryphal) response to the question

---

*Patrick Manning, "Gutenberg-e: Electronic Entry to the Historical Professoriate," *American Historical Review*, 109 (December 2004), 1506.

**Sanford G. Thatcher, "From the University Presses—A Post-Mortem for Gutenberg-e: Or, Why Ross Atkinson's Dream Is Still a Dream," *Against the Grain* (December 2008–January 2009), 72.

about the significance of the French Revolution: "It's too early to tell." Did Gutenberg-e run into difficulties because of flaws in its design or because it was ahead of its time? I favor the latter interpretation, although I, of course, am biased. I think that Gutenberg-e worked as an experiment and that it would be workable today as a sustainable enterprise. A growing population of digital natives finds it natural to read on machines. Many of their elders have become familiar with clicking around in texts and with pursuing arguments through links rather than by turning pages in consecutive order. Although the printed codex continues to dominate the market place, it no longer commands authority as the only possible kind of book. Experimentation continues with all sorts of digital and hybrid forms. Meanwhile, if any lessons are to be learned from Gutenberg-e, they should take account of the documentary evidence. I therefore think it worthwhile to publish the following two documents, which illustrate what the consensus was at the time—regarding initial ambitions for Gutenberg-e and its use for scholarship—and what it was five years later.

1. THE GRANT PROPOSAL OF 1997

The American Historical Association requests support for a three-year program to promote the publication of high-quality electronic monographs. It would organize a nation-wide competition for six prizes, to be awarded each year for the best dissertations in fields where the monograph appears to be endangered—that is, fields or sub-disciplines in which presses are reluctant to publish. One prize would be reserved for the best dissertation or first-book manuscript

by an independent historian—that is, someone whose research, unlike that of full-time faculty, is not supported by
an institution. The prize would consist of a $20,000 fel-
lowship to be used for the perfection of the book and of the
publication itself, which would be prepared by a university
press, transmitted through the World Wide Web, and accessed primarily through site licenses in research libraries,
although it might also be available in pay-per-view stations.

Purpose

The program is not intended simply to reward excellence in
scholarship with yet another prestigious prize but rather to
use prestige—the bluest of ribbons awarded by the grand-
est of juries with the full authority of the AHA behind it—
to set a high standard for electronic publishing. We also
hope to encourage scholarship in fields where university
presses are having trouble covering their costs, and we want
to help younger scholars who are finding it difficult to break
into print. By legitimizing electronic publishing, the AHA
may break down the resistance of tenure committees and
others who refuse to consider electronic publications as real
books. And by making the most of the medium, it may contribute to a new conception of the book itself as a vehicle
of knowledge.

Design

The AHA would announce the prize competition in its Web
site, in its own publications, notably *Perspectives*, its
monthly newsletter, and in other periodicals such as the
Chronicle of Higher Education. Using its listserv, which links

it to nearly every history department in the country, it would invite the chair of every department with a PhD program to nominate either one or two dissertations defended within the last three years. It also would invite applications from independent and public historians by working with organizations like the National Council on Public History, the National Coalition of Independent Scholars, and the National Adjunct Faculty Guild.

The competition will be restricted each year to areas of historical scholarship in which it has been difficult to publish monographs. Those areas will be:

In 1999: Colonial Latin America, Africa, and South Asia
In 2000: Europe before 1800
In 2001: Diplomatic and military history, not primarily in the U.S.

A panel of three senior historians will judge the entries. If necessary, they may send some of the texts for review to specialists, whom they can identify from the data base of reviewers kept by the *American Historical Review*. But they will arrive at their own decisions and explain the reasons for them in prize citations, which will function in effect as readers' reports for the publisher of the winning dissertations. The judges will produce a ranked short list of the winners, so that if the first author on the list declined the prize—that is, preferred to publish in the conventional manner—it could go to the next author, and so on down the line. The authors would commit themselves to publish their work electronically by a contract signed with a university press, which the AHA would select as the publisher of the entire series, but the contract could provide for later publication in codex form. A small number of copies would also be printed and bound for gifts and reviewing. Throughout the selection process, the dominant consideration should be the excellence of the work. The reports of the panels would serve as a guarantee that the prize books satisfied the highest standards of professional judgment.

The AHA would celebrate the winners with a great deal of fanfare at its annual meeting, and it would publicize their work extensively in its publications. They would receive a $20,000 fellowship with the understanding that they would devote the money to the preparation of the best possible electronic book. They could buy a semester's leave from their university and do some additional research. But they would be expected to concentrate on rewriting the text and on adapting it to the electronic format under the guidance of special editors at the university press.

In order to transform the raw dissertations and "final" drafts into finished books, we would want to make the most of what university presses refer to as "value added"—that is, their editorial work, copy reading, and design as well as electronic expertise. Seen from the viewpoint of a press, this experience could also have advantages, because it might open the way toward the development or improvement of an electronic publishing program. We hope, in fact, that the benefits would spread through the publishing industry as well as the academic world. But to maximize the benefits, we have been advised against distributing the monographs among several presses or creating a consortium of presses. Therefore, we propose to entrust the program to one university press, one that would be willing to make an important commitment to it. This publisher would receive a subvention, which it could spend in whatever manner it judged to be effective, such as hiring and training staff. We would favor a three-year arrangement in order to provide continuity and build up a special list: the AHA Prize Monograph Series published with the imprint of the university press. The press would handle marketing and selling; and it also would be responsible for the delivery of the work, although that technical function could be delegated to the Research Library Group (RLG).

Whether done by the university press or RLG, the delivery functions would include the following:

1. *Guidelines for authors:* the development of a style sheet to guide authors and editors in standardized markup consistent with a document-type definition (DTD).
2. *Design of an electronic space:* a storage, search, and retrieval mechanism with the possibility of links to other documents and data bases. Readers must be able to navigate within the document, and browsers on the Web should be able to consult a synopsis, a table of contents, and perhaps a sample chapter.
3. *Delivery and sales:* we expect the university press, as publisher, to sell the package of six prize books to research libraries for a set fee, leaving the libraries to arrange printing for their readers. RLG could serve as an intermediary, providing access control, scheduling fees, and managing license arrangements. But the press may prefer to handle these functions itself and also to make provision for pay-per-view reading. This aspect of the program should remain flexible. The technology is changing rapidly, and recent experience with innovations like DocuTech suggest that the printing and binding problems can be solved in the near future.

4. *Cataloguing:* RLG can guarantee that the monographs are correctly catalogued and that the catalog information is diffused through bibliographic utilities like RLIN, which it owns and operates.

5. *Archiving:* RLG backs up its online files and stores offline copies in secure, remote sites. This function is especially important, because libraries have not yet developed a secure means of preserving electronic texts.

The university press should be free to decide whether or not to delegate these functions to RLG. However they are handled, they should provide valuable experience in the development and costing of infrastructure.

Additional Elements

The electronic prize monographs should serve as a pilot project, which would provide information about the feasibility of electronic publishing throughout the social sciences and humanities. As such, it should be coordinated with the broader program now being developed by the American Council of Learned Societies, and it could be extended or expanded in different directions. For example, the AHA and the ACLS could recruit some eminent historians to publish electronic monographs in tandem with the prize books. If a Bernard Bailyn or a Natalie Davis agreed to do so, they would contribute mightily to the legitimizing function at the heart of this proposal. The inducement in such cases would not be money but rather the opportunity of helping to create a new kind of book, one with extensive documentary linkages and navigating possibilities.

It also might be possible to connect the prize books with other AHA publications, making them all available to libraries as a single package wrapped together by electronic links. These publications could include: a new individual member directory covering 15,000 historians and carefully indexed to include all current research; the AHA *Guide to Historical Literature*, currently published by the Oxford University Press; the AHA pamphlet series, now being published individually by the AHA and in book form by the Temple University Press; *Perspectives*; reprints of reviews from the *American Historical Review* (or reprints accompanied by special review essays in an "AHA Review of Books"); and perhaps back-list or out-of-print works. Of course, all such projects would involve complex negotiations with owners of copyright; but they could be mutually reinforcing, making a whole much greater and more viable financially than the sum of its parts.

We mention these possibilities, not as ingredients of the present program but as potential elements that might be grafted onto it in the future or that might be incorporated into other programs—of the ACLS or of other agencies such as the Association of Research Libraries and the National Science Foundation, which are also attempting to promote electronic publishing (two programs currently being developed are known as Building Blocks and Historical Studies Distribution Network). At this stage in the development of the AHA prize program, it seems preferable to keep the monographs relatively simple. The judges should concentrate on selecting scholarship of the highest quality, and the authors should be encouraged to convert their dissertations into electronic books in a straightforward manner—that is, without elaborate links to documents and data bases, or "bells and whistles," according to the jargon of the e-people.

Time Frame

Last January the Council of the AHA approved a preliminary version of this program, which also had been cleared through the various divisions and committees of the AHA. Joseph Miller, President of the AHA, then appointed a committee of ten, chaired by Robert Darnton, President-Elect, to study all aspects of the program and to come up with a final version. The committee, composed of representatives from university presses, libraries, RLG, and research scholarship, held extensive discussions by e-mail and telephone. Five of its members wrote position papers on the most difficult questions. Those papers generated a further discussion and the agenda for a meeting, which was held in Washington on October 10. Despite some disagreement over details, the meeting produced a clear consensus on the general shape of the program. The current proposal expresses that consensus, modified by a final round of debate among six publishers: Sanford Thatcher, Penn State Press; Colin Day, University of Michigan Press; Kate Wittenberg, Columbia University Press; John Ackerman, Cornell University Press; Lynne Withey, University of California Press; and Edward Barry, Oxford University Press.

If funding is obtained, this program will be submitted for approval by Council at the AHA meeting next January. Because Council has been informed at every stage of the process, it seems unlikely that the program will encounter serious opposition. Therefore, the competition could be announced early in 1999, and the prizes could be awarded to the winners at the AHA meeting in Chicago in January 2000. The first books might be published a year after that.

To be sure, this calendar does not leave much time for assessing as well as developing the program. Some method of assessment seems desirable, perhaps a report by an independent committee or the Association of American University Presses (AAUP). Even so, it may take several years before it is possible to judge whether the prize program provides a model worthy of emulation in other disciplines and by other publishers. We can accomplish a great deal in three years, but we may well want to apply for a renewal of the grant in 2001.

Issues and Problems

The multiple purposes of the program—to promote electronic publishing, rescue the endangered monograph, and ease the difficulties of young scholars—correspond to a set of problems that interlock at the center of academic life. Those problems concern library budgets, university presses, and the tenure process; but they cannot be unlocked by a single device. If it relieves pressure in one area, our proposal may make life easier in the others; but it also raises the danger of trying to do too many things at once or of working at cross purposes. Several members of the committee warned about the need to define priorities, and the committee as a whole thought that the development of first-rate electronic monographs should stand out as our top priority.

When the committee began its work, we believed we could easily identify the fields in which the monograph is endangered. Sanford Thatcher of the Penn State Press took an informal poll of fourteen university press directors. He confirmed that presses were reluctant to publish in fields such as African and colonial Latin American history. But he turned up so many exceptions to this rule that he concluded no field could be written off entirely as a disaster area. One press director explained, "Over half of everything that is worth doing is endangered." But neither he nor any other publisher could measure degrees of endangerment with much precision or assign them with much accuracy to specific fields. In fact, the very notion of fixed and stable fields now looks dubious. A book about popular religion in seventeenth-century Peru, which belongs on the face of it to an extremely endangered field, colonial Latin America, might sell well among students of religion, popular culture, and anthropology. Peter Givler, President of the AAUP, confirmed this view of the difficulties and warned that the AAUP would not complete its current survey of the endangered fields in the near future. If the AAUP produces a clear map of fields, marked off by warning signs about danger, we could modify our program accordingly. For the present, however, we think it best to concentrate on a few areas where the difficulties are greatest and to avoid subjects that are flourishing on the market place, such as modern America, the Civil War, and gender studies.

The committee also debated what it called the "critical-mass" issue raised by the problems of marketing the books. The publishers and librarians on the committee warned that a half-dozen books on subjects scattered over the entire historiographical landscape might not look tempting to buyers in research libraries, especially if the price were high. A series limited to a single subject—Renaissance studies, for example—would probably appeal to an acquisitions bibliographer in a research library, but we want to spread the subjects around enough to attract a broad constituency within the history profession. By restricting the competition to two fields and changing the fields each year, we hope to satisfy the needs for both focus and diversity. We have no illusions about proposing a set of texts with enough affinities in subject matter to create hypertext links within the group of prize winners. (According to one rule of thumb, it takes 500 books in a data base before readers benefit from online cross-searching.) But if this works as a pilot project, it could open the way for other, larger endeavors such as the program to be developed by the ACLS. In the long run, we should be able to develop some important linkage.

At this moment, however, we stand at the starting line of a short run, and we are certain to encounter difficulties. In fact, we have already encountered them. Three kept reappearing in our discussions with publishers: 1. Despite some useful experiments, this sort of enterprise has not been adequately tested and involves a great deal of guesswork. 2. The best-informed guesses are mutually inconsistent, at least in some important details. 3. Despite their discrepancies, all estimates indicate that electronic monographs could be expensive to produce, especially if they are heavily loaded with bells and whistles. But the Columbia University Press, which has considerable experience with electronic publishing, assures us that it can produce a lean and viable program. Its estimates form the basis for the budget that follows.

What to conclude? We dare not make promises about black ink and bottom lines. But we can put together a feasible program, one that will provide a start toward solving a set of problems at the heart of scholarly life in this country. At the very least, this program will generate the knowledge necessary to get a better understanding of those problems. But we expect it to do more. It should open the way to a new kind of scholarly communication, the well-wrought electronic monograph. Some variety of electronic book seems certain to proliferate in the near future, but it will be done well only if an organization like the AHA takes the lead in developing it, setting standards, and legitimizing the whole endeavor in the eyes of a skeptical profession.

Robert Darnton
President-Elect, American Historical Association

2. THE PROGRESS REPORT OF 2002

Now that the Gutenberg-e program has reached the half-way point of its six-year life span, I can offer some reflections on its progress. We launched the first e-books at the American Historical Association meeting last month in San Francisco. It was a happy moment. Superb presentations by two of the winners from our first class, Ignacio Gallup-Diaz and Michael Katten, combined with the announcement of the new winners, who make up our third class, produced a mood of triumphalism. That, of course, is dangerous. I think we may indulge in a modest amount of self-congratulation, but we have encountered problems. I would like to discuss them, and our proposals for solving them, leaving the details of the year's activities to the report by the AHA staff, which follows these remarks.

From the beginning in 1998, we intended to set a fast pace and to aim high. I now think that the pace may have been too fast. The first competition took place in 1999; the first winners were announced in January 2000; the first workshops were held in 2000–2001; and the first e-books were published in January 2002. But there were only two of them. True, a third book was submitted in January, and a fourth should be

completed by March. Moreover, those who missed the deadline had valid excuses (in one case, a son who came down
with cancer, in another a pregnancy and childbirth). But I
think the deadline set by Columbia University Press—originally
one year, extended to two—was not realistic. The winners
face the difficulties of publishing their first book while cop-
ing with many other demands, such as finding a job, moving
house, preparing their first lectures, and founding families.
We therefore decided to set a two-year deadline and to be
flexible. There will not be an annual "launch" of six e-books,
but Columbia will put them online as they become available.
Some, in fact, will be finished ahead of time. Greg Brown
from class three is only weeks away from submitting his final
text, which will be published before some of the e-books from
class one. Now that the first books have appeared, Columbia
will turn out a continuous stream of products. That may create some difficulties for its marketing department, which had
planned to sell an annual packet of six books (the current
price is $195 for all six, very inexpensive, in my view). But
there are ways around that obstacle. For my part, I think I
made the mistake of setting the stakes too high. In the first
years, I stressed the innovative potential of e-books as a new
form of scholarly communication, and the first winners probably felt compelled to come up with something too elaborate
to be feasible within a short time. In subsequent pep talks
with the winners, I stressed the importance of sheer quality
and the need to avoid the temptation of "bells and whistles"
(please forgive that tired metaphor).

The second problem concerns our high aims. We tried to
do too many things at once: to help solve the problem of the
threatened monograph, to create a new kind of book, to legitimize it in the eyes of the history profession, to help young

historians get over the first hurdle in their careers, and to favor independent historians who do not have teaching positions in higher education. Instead of being deluged with applications, as I had expected, we received relatively few dissertations in each of the first three years. As the deadline for last year's competition approached, we had only four submissions. We rescheduled things, broadened the scope of the competition, and soon found ourselves with forty competitors. In the end, we were happy with the result—but chastised. I now believe it is best to concentrate on producing excellent e-books, the sort that will set a standard and that will legitimize the medium at the same time. We therefore plan to enlarge the scope of the next competitions instead of restricting them to the fields in which it is most difficult to publish.

A third problem concerns the administration of the program. Last year the AHA Council voted to take the day-to-day supervision of Gutenberg-e out of my hands and to assign it to the Research Division under the direction of an AHA vice president. I don't think anyone was dissatisfied with my stewardship, but there was a sense that instead of being Darnton's pet project, Gutenberg-e should be folded into the normal operations of the Association. That decision suited me, because Gutenberg-e has occupied a vast amount of my time and energy for the last four years. I retired into the background as a member of a supervisory committee, whose main function is to choose the topics and the judges for the annual competition. But despite excellent work by the AHA staff, no one coordinated all the aspects of the program. There are a lot of them, and minor hitches are always snagging things. Therefore, at the San Francisco meeting we decided to remove the management of the program from the Research Division and to assign it to the executive director of the AHA, Arnita

Jones. Arnita appreciates how important Gutenberg-e is to the AHA, and she has promised to devote a great deal of her considerable energy to making it work. She also has hired a half-time assistant with a history PhD to help with the daily tasks. I think this solution is perfect, and I shall continue to participate actively in the program as a member of the supervisory committee.

The details of the year's activities can be studied from the narrative and financial reports, which follow. I would like to mention only one final issue: What is to become of this initiative after the program comes to an end in January 2005? (Of course, given the extension of the deadline, the last e-books will be published by January 2007.) Be assured, I am not going to ask for a renewal. But I think the AHA should capitalize on the success of the program—and it clearly is successful, even at this early stage—in order to establish electronic publishing as a legitimate form of communicating knowledge. Although my ideas are somewhat vague at this point, I think the AHA should use its new History Cooperative Web Site to create a series that could be called "The History Cooperative Monographs." It should publish first-rate dissertations without restriction as to field or number, but it should guarantee their quality by submitting them to a panel of well-qualified judges. There might be several panels, each representing a general field of study, or perhaps the editorial board of the *American Historical Review* could supervise the refereeing, thereby extending its gatekeeper function in the vetting of articles. The dissertations could be published in their current form, or they could be reworked as e-books. But they needn't involve the elaborate editorial and electronic transformation that has characterized the Gutenberg-e-books. Columbia University Press should be given the opportunity of publishing the series itself, if it wanted to continue the Gutenberg-e initiative in another form, one that would involve less editing and more dissertations. Or the Illinois University Press, which is a partner in the History Cooperative, might want to be the publisher. Many possibilities need to be explored, and many problems, including financing, need to be solved. Whatever happens, we should devise some kind of follow-up for Gutenberg-e, and we should be thinking now about a future that is only four years away.

Robert Darnton
Past President, American Historical Association

CHAPTER 7

Open Access

The following short essay was intended to state the case for open access just before a vote on an open-access resolution by the Faculty of Arts and Sciences at Harvard University. It was published by the Harvard Crimson *on February 12, 2008, and on the same day the resolution was carried unanimously. Since then similar resolutions have been adopted by other faculties at Harvard and by other universities.*

THE MOTION BEFORE the Faculty of Arts and Sciences in support of open access to scholarly articles concerns openness in general. It is meant to promote the free communication of knowledge. By retaining rights for the widest possible dissemination of the faculty's work, it would make scholarship by members of the FAS freely accessible everywhere in the world, and it would reinforce a new effort by Harvard to share its intellectual wealth.

The university library has taken a leading role in that endeavor. Far from reserving its resources for the privileged few, it is digitizing its special collections, opening them to everyone online, and cooperating with Google in the attempt to make books in the public domain actually available to the public, a worldwide public, which extends everywhere that people have access to the Internet. If the FAS votes in favor of the motion on February 12, Harvard will make the latest work of its scholars accessible, just as it is creating accessibility to the store of knowledge that it has accumulated in its libraries since 1638.

The motion also represents an opportunity to reshape the landscape of learning. A shift in the system for communicating knowledge has created a contradiction at the heart of academic life. We academics provide the content for scholarly journals. We evaluate articles as referees, we serve on editorial boards, we work as editors ourselves, yet the journals force us to buy back our work, in published form, at outrageous prices. Many journals now cost more than $20,000 for a year's subscription.

The spiraling cost of journals has inflicted severe damage on research libraries, creating a ripple effect: in order to purchase the journals, libraries have had to reduce their acquisitions of monographs; the reduced demand among libraries for monographs has forced university presses to cut back on the publication of them; and the near impossibility of publishing their dissertations has jeopardized the careers of a whole generation of scholars in many fields. It would be naive to assume that a positive vote by the FAS on February 12 would force publishers to slash their prices. But by passing the motion we can begin to resist the trends that have created so much damage.

Of course, we faculty members do not pay the high cost of journals ourselves. We expect our libraries to do it—with all the negative consequences that I have mentioned. The motion before the FAS provides a way to realign the means of communication in a way that will favor learning. It will be a first step toward freeing scholarship from the stranglehold of commercial publishers by making it freely available on our own university repository. Instead of being the passive victims of the system, we can seize the initiative and take charge of it.

Although this initiative is being submitted to the Faculty of Arts and Sciences, it concerns all the faculties of the university. All of them face the same problems. Harvard Medical School, for example, is working on ways to help its faculty members comply with the recent legislation by Congress mandating that all articles based on research funded by the National Institutes of Health be made openly accessible through PubMed Central, the data base maintained by the National Library of Medicine.

The Harvard University Library will set up an Office for Scholarly Communication to make the open-access repository an instrument for access to research across all disciplines in the spirit of the "one-university" environment that the electronic HOLLIS catalog now provides for holdings in all the libraries, more than ninety of them, throughout the university system. The Office for Scholarly Communication will also promote maximum cooperation by the faculty. Many repositories already exist in other universities, but they have failed to get a large proportion of faculty members to submit their articles. The deposit rate at the University of California is 14 percent, and it is much lower in most other places. By mandating copyright retention and by placing those rights in the hands of the institution running the repository, the motion will create the conditions for a high deposit rate.

What further sets Harvard's proposal apart from the others is its opt-out provision. Whereas other repositories depend on faculty opting in by volunteering to provide digitized copies of their work, the Harvard system would have all faculty members grant a non-exclusive license to the President and Fellows of Harvard to make their articles freely available online through the open-access repository. The system would be collective but not coercive. Anyone could comply with a journal's demand for an exclusive right to an article by obtaining a waiver, which will be granted automatically. Of course, those who cooperate with the system will also retain full rights to the publication of their work. By sharing those rights with Harvard, they sacrifice nothing; and they will have the collective weight of Harvard behind them if they resist a journal's demand for exclusive rights. We have designed a legal memorandum called an author's addendum to reinforce them in negotiations with commercial publishers.

The implementation of the proposal would require an effort at consciousness-raising, but that, too, is a good cause, because few faculty members understand how badly current conditions impede the communication of knowledge. The motion gives Harvard the possibility of setting an example that could spread. In place of a closed, privileged, and costly system, it will help open up the world of learning to everyone who wants to learn—and also to contribute to learning, because the Office for Scholarly Communication could point the way toward a digital commonwealth, in which ideas would flow freely in all directions. Harvard's motion represents only one step toward this goal. But it shows how the new technology can make it possible to realize an old ideal, a republic of letters in which citizenship extends to everyone.

PART III

Past

CHAPTER 8

A Paean to Paper

This essay, published in 2001, describes a world we have lost, a world in which news was attached to paper and the newspaper provided citizens with their basic diet of information. Since then newspapers have begun to disappear. Because they depend on advertising and advertising has migrated to the Internet, they frequently cannot cover their costs. News now appears online, often in short messages exchanged among nonprofessionals acting as reporters. It used to be written for the general reader. Now it is written by the general reader.

Yet the paean to paper in Nicholson Baker's Double Fold, *which provided the occasion for this essay, remains relevant in the age of the Internet. Baker deplored the substitution of microfilm for newspapers and books. Today we rely on digitization, even though digital copies are more vulnerable than microfilm to decay and obsolescence. Librarians increasingly acquire material "born digital" or in digital formats, yet they have no safe method of preserving it. Paper is still the best medium of preservation, and libraries still need to fill their shelves with words printed on paper. Moreover, digitization as performed in Google Book Search can be every bit as faulty as microfilming was four decades ago. As a cautionary tale,* Double Fold *deserves pondering, because it raises issues that refuse to go away.*

WHEN JOURNALISTS DISCUSS their craft, they invoke contradictory clichés: "Today's newspaper is the first draft of history," and "Nothing is more dead than yesterday's newspaper." Both in a way are true: news feeds history with facts, yet most of it is forgotten. Suppose newspapers disappeared from libraries: would history vanish from the collective memory? That is the disaster that Nicholson Baker denounces in *Double Fold: Libraries and the Assault on Paper*, a *j'accuse* pointed at the library profession.

Librarians have purged their shelves of newspapers, he argues, because they are driven by a misguided obsession about saving space. And they have deluded themselves into believing that nothing has been lost, because they have replaced the papers with microfilm. The microfilm, however, is inadequate, incomplete, faulty, and frequently illegible. Worse, it was never needed in the first place, because contrary to another common delusion, the papers were not disintegrating on the shelves. Despite their chemistry—acids working on wood-pulp in paper manufactured after 1870—they have held up very well. And now the paper massacre has spread to books. They, too, are being sold off, thrown away, and hideously damaged in harebrained experiments to preserve them. The custodians of our culture are destroying it.

As jeremiads go, this is an odd one. Wickedness has provided material for lamentation in America since the days of the Puritans. But instead of ranting against the whore of

Babylon, Baker aims his indignation at Marian the Librarian—not, of course, the small-time, small-town keepers of books, but their high-minded, high-flying superiors: Patricia Battin, for example, formerly the librarian of Columbia University, who led the "assault on paper" from the Commission on Preservation and Access and received an award from President Clinton in 1999 for "saving history." Baker indicts her for destroying history and makes her into one of the chief villains of his book. The others come from foundations (Ford, Mellon), research libraries (Yale, Chicago), the National Endowment for the Humanities, and above all the Library of Congress.

They make a strange cast of characters: butchers of books from the unlikely world of libraries. Baker describes them as civil, cultivated, and generally genial—the unassuming types you would expect to encounter behind old oak desks in book-lined studies. Making the most of his novelist's touch, he introduces each character with telling bits of description. They wear "quiet silk scarves," bow ties, and understated suits. They gaze out at you from beneath "wise-looking eyebrows" and "cheerfully bald" foreheads or through "large, rectilinear glasses similar to those Joyce Carol Oates used to wear in pictures." Such gentle souls could not possibly be vandals, you tell yourself. And that response puts you under the spell of Baker's rhetoric, because he tries to show that the barbarians are not at the gate: they are already in the temple, destroying its treasures and doing so all the more effectively because they pad about in sensible shoes and tweed.

The rhetoric fuels the argument, but what is the argument itself, stripped down to a set of propositions? It goes as follows:

1. *Paper holds up well, even the cheapest paper made for pulp fiction from pulped wood according to the manufacturing processes developed after 1850.* Baker goes over the chemistry of acidification, conceding minor points: paper with a low pH tends to be weaker than less acidic paper, and newspapers laced with alum-rosin will turn yellow if over-exposed to light. But he carries his main point: despite prophecies of doom, paper made in the late nineteenth century has not disintegrated; it can be read today without undergoing damage, and there is no reason to believe that it will not last another hundred years.

2. *Microfilm is not an adequate substitute for paper.* Its chemistry is worse. Frames that were supposed to last forever have developed blemishes and bubbles. They have faded into illegibility. They have torn and shrunk and sprouted fungi and emitted foul odors and melted together on the spool into solid lumps of cellulose. Microfilmed runs of newspapers often contain gaps where the technicians skipped pages or failed to adjust the focus. The work has been so botched that librarians have proclaimed sets to be "complete" if they lack six percent of their issues. And the sets are hideously expensive. During the first wave of "preservation" through microfilming, the State Library of Pennsylvania and the Free Library of Philadelphia stripped their shelves of complete runs of the *Philadelphia Inquirer*. A set on microfilm now costs $621,515.

Reading microfilms is hell. Hours spent cranking blurry images under a hot light and staring at a screen can turn you off research and even turn your stomach. Baker reports that a microfilm reader in the Archives of Ontario had an air-sickness bag attached to it. Sickening or not, microfilmed copies of newspapers are all we have in many cases, and they are often incomplete. Entire years are missing from important newspapers, and there are no complete sets of the originals anywhere in existence, because librarians have got rid of them. Baker puts it polemically: "A million people a day once read Pulitzer's *World*; now an original set is a good deal rarer than a Shakespeare First Folio or the Gutenberg Bible." Baker is polemical, but he is right.

3. Librarians crave space. To them, space, like time, is money; and money is scarce, because their budgets are beleaguered. Yet the newspapers and books continue to pour in, their output growing inexorably year after year. Marian feels like the sorcerer's apprentice. How can she stop the flood? Find the shelving? Fund extensions and annexes? The obvious answer is miniaturization: replace tomes with microtexts, throw away the originals, and expand the library's holdings while keeping its shelf space constant. Baker shows how this notion captured the imagination of the country's leading librarians and led to the stripping of shelves—"deaccessioning" in the sanitized jargon of library science. He makes the point effectively, quoting from speeches, memos, and professional journals. But then he goes further:

4. The obsession with space degenerated into an "ideology." Driven by the "fear of demon Growth," key librarians have "demonized old paper." They hate the stuff and want to get rid of it at all costs—costs so high that they could trigger a revolt of tax payers, to say nothing of book lovers. To fend off this danger, the nation's leading librarians have spread a panic about the self-destructive quality of paper and then promoted technologies for destroying it in the name of preservation. Here, I think, Baker stretches his argument beyond believability. Instead of providing a credible explanation of what drove librarians to strip shelves, he makes them into villains and does some demonizing of his own—covered up with details about quiet scarves and bow ties. Nonetheless, he carries a crucial point:

5. *Preservation meant destruction.* Not always, of course. Some institutions like the Boston Public Library never harmed their collections. Some, like the New York Public Library, retained some sets of newspapers after microfilming them. But the Library of Congress took the lead in a book-and-newspaper massacre of staggering proportions. In order to microfilm works printed after 1870, the Library adopted a policy of "disbinding" them—that is, splitting them down their spines so they could be splayed open and photographed efficiently. Although it can be saved, an unbound volume, especially of old newspapers, generally gets trashed. If they don't throw them away, libraries sell them off, often at absurdly low prices, and they find buyers—not as a rule among readers who would save the work but among businessmen intent on destroying it further. Baker talked himself into the warehouse of Historic Newspaper Archives, Inc., a 25,000-square-foot structure crammed with newspapers, which are cut apart and shipped out to people who want a memento of their birthday or some other event. He found a monumental set of the *New York Herald Tribune* in mint condition, which, he surmises, had been given for safe keeping to the New York Public Library by the Trib's owner, Mrs. Ogden Reid. It was being gutted for souvenirs, and Baker managed to buy two weeks' worth of 1934 for $300.

6. *The destruction was unnecessary.* From 1957, the Council on Library Resources, founded by Verner Clapp, the second in command at the Library of Congress, sponsored experiments to determine the longevity of wood-pulp paper. The experimenters stripped paper out of books printed be-

tween 1900 and 1950 and attempted to age it artificially by folding it back and forth in a specially designed machine. After ten years and 500 ruined books, they concluded that most printed matter from the first half of the twentieth century would not make it to the year 2000. The anticipated body count came to 1.75 billion pages, more than enough to spread panic among the keepers of the country's research libraries.

In order to estimate the mortality rate in their own collections, the librarians used a simplified version of the paper test: they folded a corner back and forth through a 180-degree arc on each side of a leaf. If the paper tore after two or three double folds—accompanied at times with some gentle tugging— it was deemed to be doomed and scheduled to be replaced by microfilm before it disintegrated on the shelf. Librarians and student helpers folded their way through 36,500 volumes at Yale. Their conclusion: 1.3 million volumes would self-destruct before the twenty-first century. Yale adopted a "slash and burn" policy of microfilming, which eliminated half the books in its great collection of American history. Those books would be there today had the librarians not fallen for the double-fold fashion, because double-folding creates creases that tear, whereas reading involves nothing more than turning pages. Pages that would flunk the double-fold test can be read hundreds of times without any damage. Books that should have disintegrated long ago, according to the most advanced library science, are still doing very nicely—except for those that the librarians destroyed in order to preserve.

7. *The destruction was brutal.* Microfilming can be done without harming volumes, by placing them in cradles and adjusting the camera to the appropriate angle. However, that

procedure takes time, and preservationists have been in such a hurry to save books and newspapers from their misdiagnosed deaths that they have killed them by "guillotining"—that is, by slicing them down their spines so that the unbound pages could be photographed rapidly lying flat. Once dismembered, most of them were pulped.

The experts in the Library of Congress and the Council on Library Resources have also guillotined books in order to experiment with techniques for deacidifying paper. Their most spectacular experiments involved a substance known as DEZ, for diethyl zinc. Potentially, DEZ could destroy acidity by creating an "alkaline buffer" in the fibers of the paper, but it has an unfortunate side effect: it bursts into flames on contact with air and explodes if exposed to water. Although it works better in bombs and missiles than in books, the Library's experimenters used it as the key ingredient in a facility intended to deacidify a million books a year. In fact, as Baker remarks, they designed "a large fuel-air bomb that happened to contain books." Sure enough, it exploded in trial runs conducted by NASA at the Goddard Space Flight Center in 1985 and 1986. Further experiments produced further disasters, until, thousands of books and millions of dollars later, the program was abandoned.

Meanwhile, however, the preservationists devised other experiments, including a million-dollar project to force rats to inhale zinc-oxide dust in order to prove that deacidified books could be sniffed without harm. Together with the microfilmers, deaccessioners, and demolition crews, they razored, guillotined, chainsawed, pickled, gassed, baked, burned, and dissolved vast quantities of printed matter. Baker may overdo the anthropomorphic verbs and slant the technical descriptions in a way that makes librarians look like mad scientists.

But he produces enough hard evidence to make a book lover's skin crawl.

8. *The destruction was expensive.* Baker comes up with plenty of examples of books and newspapers that were discarded or sold at derisive prices by libraries and then sold again for hefty sums by dealers. He also documents instances where it cost more to buy the microfilm of a book than the original. And after citing case after case of expensive solutions to misconceived problems, he proposes a relatively cheap and simple solution of his own: store the originals in air-conditioned warehouses, where they will last indefinitely. Short of that, do nothing: "Leave the books alone, I say, leave them alone, leave them alone." But the librarians preferred to spend vast sums in order to comply with the orthodoxy of their profession: microfilm and discard. What was the cost? Baker estimates that American libraries got rid of 975,000 books worth $39 million. The economics of the whole business seems as whacky as the science.

The cultural loss cannot be estimated. Libraries usually began to strip their shelves of newspapers with issues dating from 1870 onward—that is, when the mass circulation dailies began to develop. By the end of the century, thanks to the cheap paper, Linotype, and high-powered printing, the newspapers of Pulitzer, Hearst, and other press barons had become a major force in American life. They brought us more than the Spanish-American War. They shaped the emergence of mass culture, consumerism, professional sports, and great stretches of American literature—produced in large part by reporters turned writers. How can historians study those subjects without reading daily newspapers? But how can they read the newspapers, if they have disappeared? Microfilm will not do, not only because it is riddled with faults and gaps but also because it fails to convey the texture of the printed page—the way headlines, layout, touches of color, and the tactile qualities of broadsheet and tabloid orient the reader and guide the eye through meaningful patches of print. According to an advertisement of University Microfilms, the stripping of newspapers from libraries was "our own slum clearance program." Baker comes closer to the truth: "This country has strip-mined a hundred and twenty years of its history."

9. *The librarians may have had good intentions, but they acted in bad faith.* Having convinced themselves that they were running out of space and that microfilming was the answer, they concocted a false crisis in order to clear their shelves. The books, they said, were burning. They used other expressions: dissolving, rotting, crumbling. "Turning to dust" was a favorite metaphor, served up with the adverb "literally" to mean that some kind of chemical combustion was consuming the books as they stood on the shelves. What kind? None of the preservationists produced an accurate analysis. No one found a single smoldering volume or ashes or evidence of any kind. No matter: *Slow Fires*, a documentary horror film commissioned by the Council on Library Resources, spread the false notion of combustibility; and false consciousness spread through the ranks of librarians, heightened by hype from their leaders, such as Patricia Battin: "80% of the materials in our libraries are published on acid paper and will inevitably crumble. The Library of Congress alone reports that 77,000 volumes in its collections move each year from the 'endangered' state to brittleness and thence to crumbs." After sufficient citation, the figure of 77,000 (or in some versions 70,000) crumbling volumes hardened into solid fact, accompanied by other firm bits of library pseudo-science:

collections doubled every sixteen years; 3.3 million volumes will disintegrate within twenty years; and it will cost $358 million to rescue them by microfilming, although the expense will actually be a savings, because it will create the possibility of freeing shelf space by getting rid of 16.5 million duplicates scattered needlessly around the country.

These nine propositions add up to a terrible indictment of a venerable profession. Are there no arguments for the defense? Instead of going over them impartially, Baker gives full vent to what he calls his "prosecutorial urge." He stacks the evidence in his favor, not by distorting it but by rhetorical devices, such as putting quotations out of context and splicing comments into them. In recounting an interview with Patricia Battin, for example, he intersperses her remarks with those of other people, which seem to refute them, and with refutations of his own. At one point, he has her tell him, "I don't think that saving space was the issue." Then he quotes an article by one of her fellow librarians at Columbia: "Think about space costs . . ." He links that quotation with an inflammatory remark about book crumbling from another passage in the same article: "The central stacks of all major libraries will soon be condemned as unsanitary landfill—the world's intellectual garbage dumps." Then he switches back to Battin: "And yet to me she said, in the sincerest possible voice, 'I don't think it's your librarians that have ever tried to miniaturize in order to save space.'" Decontextualization of this kind produces guilt by association.

Producing guilt is the object of the prosecutorial urge; but in his determination to damn some of the country's most eminent librarians, Baker sometimes muddles the issues. Space is a serious problem for librarians, not one that they attempt to conjure away by "demonization" or by giving free rein to some psychic loathing of paper. Paper can be fragile. Books are often damaged. Microfilming does preserve at least some of the historical record, even if it cannot be an adequate substitute for the original works. Libraries no longer guillotine books in order to microfilm them, and they no longer throw away the originals. Most of Baker's horror stories date from an era that has passed, leaving a trail of destruction, to be sure, but also a reaction against its misguided policies. After some scandals about the loss of precious books, the New York Public Library committed itself to a strong stand against deaccessioning; and other libraries have followed suit. Not that the danger has disappeared. Baker rightly warns that the enthusiasm for digitizing could produce another purge of paper. But he lavishes most of his indignation on practices that have been abandoned.

The *j'accuse* genre does not work well when applied to the past. It is better suited to journalism than to history. In its original form, Baker's polemic appeared as a journalistic essay in the *New Yorker*; and it succeeded splendidly, because it linked the malpractices of libraries to a current scandal. The British Library had been clearing its shelves of its fabulous collection of late nineteenth- and twentieth-century American newspapers; and speculators were buying them up at trivial prices in order to dismember them and sell them off as souvenirs. When Baker got wind of the devastation, he tried desperately to stop it. But the Library would not listen, would not even give him and other bibliophiles time to mount a rescue operation. In the end, a priceless treasure was squandered, a public trust betrayed, and a small portion of the collection survived, because Baker himself bought it, after cashing in his savings and forming a not-for-profit corporation with the help of a few foundations. Complete, uncrumbled runs of the *World*, the *Herald Tribune*, and other great dailies now sit safely in a storage facility that Baker constructed near his house in Maine. "Sometimes I'm a little stunned to think that I've become a newspaper librarian, more or less, and have the job of watching over this majestic, pulp-begotten ancestral stockpile," he concluded. It's a great story, told with zest and humor: Don Quixote tilting against the British Library and winning at least one round. But it does not make for great history.

When Baker expanded the *New Yorker* piece into a book, he faced the problem of blending his story into a general account of library stewardship in the United States since World War II. He cut the text from the *New Yorker* in two and used both parts, virtually unchanged, as the first chapters and conclusion to the book. In between, he sandwiched a historical narrative. But it was not conventional history. The text did not follow a chronological order or any clear organizational pattern at all. Instead, it consisted of vignettes, brief, brilliant essays strung together in a way that would stun the reader and stoke the indignation as one bizarre episode followed another.

Implicit in it all, however, was an argument about institutional change, which can be summarized as follows. In 1944, an influential librarian named Fremont Rider propounded a "natural law" of library growth. It seemed to prove by impressive mathematical formulas that America's libraries were hurtling into a spectacular space crisis. The only solution, according to Rider, lay in the technology developed by the Office of Strategic Services during World War II: books could be replaced by microcards or some other product of miniaturization. Verner Clapp, the number two man at the Library of Congress, took up the cause and proselytized from the Council on Library Resources, where he became director in 1956. During more than thirty years at the summit of the library world, Clapp promoted experiments in "preservation" that led to the microfilming and loss of millions of newspapers and books. From 1968 to 1984, the Preservation and Microfilming Office of the Library of Congress filmed ninety-three million pages and "threw out more than ten million dollars' worth of public property."

It took some effort, however, to persuade the leaders of the other great research libraries that preservation did not mean keeping books. So Clapp's successor at the Council, Warren Haas, mounted a PR offensive, and he enlisted Patricia Battin, the powerful head librarian at Columbia University, to spread propaganda from the Commission on Preservation and Access. By articles, lectures, colloquia, Congressional hearings, *Slow Fires*, and gossip through grapevines, they spread the word that the country's libraries would turn to dust, if the shelves were not purged of paper and filled with film. They perpetrated the double-fold test, just the thing to justify the librarians' desire to save space by getting rid of books. The microfilming and deaccessioning frenzy came to a climax in the 1980s. But the tide turned around 1994, when Patricia Battin retired from the Commission. A reaction set in, led by sensible bibliographers like G. Thomas Tanselle, and the annihilation of the newspapers at the British Library provided a final scandal, which brought the story to a close in 1999.

As stories go, it is surprisingly simple. Misguided zealots misdiagnosed a problem, and produced a national catastrophe by spreading misinformation. The disparity between cause and effect cries out for explanation. What fundamentally was at work in the process—sheer stupidity? flaws in institutions? the influence of one or two powerful personalities and the appeal of a few striking ideas? Questions of that sort differentiate history from journalism. Baker does not ask them; he merely points his finger at the guilty parties. But there is an interpretation implicit in the finger-pointing.

A surprising number of the villains in the plot turn out to have some connection with the CIA, Operations Research, missile defense, the Pentagon, or a branch of the military-industrial complex. Baker emphasizes that the obsession with microfilming developed, like the CIA itself, from the Office of Strategic Services during World War II. Verner Clapp spread it from the Library of Congress while secretly "a consultant of the CIA," and the line of consultants leads right up to the present librarian, James Billington, whose CIA connection is flagged in a long and rather irrelevant endnote. The "war scientists and CIA consultants" were thickest on the ground at the Council on Library Resources—so thick, in fact, that Baker's poker-faced summaries of their CVs suggests a Dr. Strangelove lurking at every water cooler.

His account of the mad experiments with book baking and DEZ conjures up something nastier—systematic annihilation, or what he calls "destroying to preserve." A quotation from the *Washington Post* evokes the same associations: "Must the Library of Congress Destroy Books to Save Them?" The reader cannot help but think of the most haunting remark from the Vietnamese War: "It was necessary to destroy the village in order to save it." And the chain of associations turns still darker, when Baker talks about "putting old books in gas chambers." Here the argument by innuendo has got out of hand. The librarians did not butcher books in the way that the Nazis annihilated people.

Should they also be condemned, as Baker claims, for destroying history? Perhaps, if newspapers really can be counted as history's first draft. Baker seems to adopt this view through the vivid use of metaphor—for example, when he describes a shipment of 4,600 volumes of the *Chicago Tribune* as "sixteen pallets, ten tons of major metropolitan history." But just as microfilms should not be confused with original documents, history should not be equated with its sources. It is an argument from evidence, not the evidence itself.

Had Baker pursued this line of thought, he could have strengthened his case; for newspapers, studied as sources, open up vast possibilities of deepening our understanding of the past. Not that they are transparent windows into a world we have lost, as Baker seems to think. They are collections of stories, written by professionals within the conventions of their craft. But if taken as stories—news stories, a peculiar kind of narrative—they convey the way contemporaries construed events and found some meaning in the booming, buzzing confusion of the world around them.

For many readers today, the front page of the *New York Times* provides a map of what happened yesterday. They read it as they read a map, for orientation—usually from right to left, or from the lead story to the off-lead, following clues from headlines, pausing over pictures, wandering below the fold or into interior pages, according to the way that they respond to suggestions from layout and typography. The editors of the *Times* take those anticipated reactions into account when they design page one every day at their 5:00 conference. An implicit dialogue develops between the producers of the cognitive map and the consumers who put it to use. The style of the stories and the conventions of the layout change over time, suggesting subtle shifts in ways of viewing the world—

nothing that can be pinned down with precision but something that undergirds experience and that historians strive to understand. They can never reach an adequate understanding, if they have to work from microfilm.

To be sure, a history of world-views requires more than careful reading of original sets of newspapers. Burckhardt and Huizinga showed the way by consulting evidence of everything from table manners and death rituals to forms of speech and styles of dress. Anthropologists have demonstrated how such material can be worked into systematic accounts of culture. But the evidence thins as the anthropologically informed historian attempts to penetrate further back in time. Chapbooks and broadsides were the most popular kind of printed matter in early modern Europe—so popular, in fact, that libraries did not deign to collect them. Historians like Robert Mandrou have picked through their remains in an effort to reconstruct *mentalités collectives*, but the result is disappointing. How will historians piece together a picture of American mentality in the Gilded Age if they have no newspapers—real newspapers, full size and in full color—to consult?

In short, Baker rightly condemns the deaccessioning of newspapers as a loss to history, even though he has an inadequate notion of what history is and he does not succeed in writing it himself. If taken as literature, however, his book is a spectacular success. As mentioned above, it belongs to a peculiar genre, the American jeremiad. But that raises problems, because Americans have been told that the sky is falling, the ocean rising, the earth quaking, the economy recessing, the presidency degrading, the family disappearing, and the cosmos running out of time. How can they work up a lather about old newspapers and books? Cows are going mad, whales are being beached, glaciers are melting, forests are burning, species are vanishing, lungs are collapsing, the ozone layer is about to go, and social welfare as we knew it has gone. Why should we get mad at librarians?

In order to whip up indignation, Baker deploys a formidable array of rhetorical devices. He has perfect pitch in his choice of narrative voice. Essentially, he adopts the tone of Innocence Abroad. How did I get into this mess? he asks the reader with false naiveté: "In 1993, I decided to write some essays on trifling topics—movie projectors, fingernail clippers, punctuation, and the history of the word 'lumber.'" Before we have a chance to ask why Baker should be writing about fingernail clippers, we are swept up in a mad tale about librarians destroying books.

Baker makes us his traveling companion in the strange world of librarianship, nudging us confidentially in the midst of interviews by parenthetical remarks and editorial comments. For example, after showing us a beautiful discarded volume of the *Chicago Tribune* with the seal of Harvard University and a bookplate proclaiming it to be purchased from the bequest of Ichabod Tucker, class of 1791, he calls up a librarian at Harvard in order to find out whether it was sold off as a duplicate. "Oh, we would never have hard copies going back that far—they just don't keep," she replies. He then shoots back, not to her but as an aside addressed to us: "They don't keep, kiddo, if you don't keep them."

The colloquialism and the gotcha mode of quoting makes us complicit with the author and eases our way through esoteric detail about chemical formulas and microphotography. After explaining how scientists devised tests and designed charts to trace a non-phenomenon, the degradation of paper, with mathematical precision, he explodes: "This is of course utter horseshit and craziness." "Right," we want to say to him. "Right on."

The esoterica matters, however, because Baker needs to establish his bona fides in the labs and to give the reader a sense of being there—"there," in the case of Library of Congress experiments, being a madhouse:

> Diethyl zinc (or DEZ, as it's jauntily acronymed) was the active ingredient in a patented technique developed at the Library of Congress in the early seventies. You arrange your acid-beset books in milk crates, spine down, up to five thousand of them at a time, and stack the crates in a ten-foot high retrofitted space-simulation chamber that bears some resemblance to a railroad tank car; then you shut the round door at the end, suck out the air, and let the miracle DEZ fog creep in.

The description has enough science to make it believable and enough parenthetical comment to make it absurd.

Baker uses the same techniques in his novels: microscopic detail, served up straight but with enough disconcerting language to make it hilarious or shocking.

Double Fold, however, presents itself as reportage. It describes real people, who receive the same hyperrealist treatment as the procedures in the labs: hence the details about dress. Chandru Shahani, chief scientist at the Library of Congress, is "a friendly man in a gray suit." Verner Clapp is "polymathic, bow tie–wearing"; Daniel Boorstin, "a chronic bow-tie wearer." (Baker seems to have a thing about bow ties.) Baker attaches descriptive tags to each person as he introduces him, and they are often favorable: "smiley, self-effacing"; "polite, plummy"; "brusque charm." While enjoying a specious sense of familiarity with the cast of characters, the reader is reassured about Baker's innocent objectivity.

The details make the indictment believable, because Baker does not ascribe evil motives to the villains of the plot. He simply records the disasters produced by their misguided policies. As Innocence Abroad, he seems to take in the entire landscape with trustworthy neutrality. His narrator's "I" is a camera. It sees through everything and exposes the whole system to be rotten.

Hyperrealism as a morality tale: it is a tour de force and a great read. But is it true? On the whole, I think it is, although it is less innocent than it seems. It should be read as a journalistic jeremiad rather than as a balanced account of library history over the last fifty years. And it also should be read for its policy recommendations. Baker makes four. All deserve support:

1. Libraries that receive public money should as a condition of funding be required to publish monthly lists of discards on their Web sites, so that the public has some way of determining which of them are acting responsibly on behalf of their collections.
2. The Library of Congress should lease or build a large building near Washington, and in it they should put, in call-number order, everything that they are sent by publishers and can't or don't want to hold on site. If the library is unwilling to perform this basic function of a national repository, then Congress should designate and fund some other archive to do the job.
3. Several libraries around the country should begin to save the country's current newspaper output in bound form.
4. The National Endowment for the Humanities should either abolish the U.S. Newspaper Program and the

Brittle Books Program entirely, or require as a condition of funding that all microfilming and digital scanning be nondestructive and that all originals be saved afterward.

What of the wonderful runs of newspapers that have disappeared from the library shelves? A few have survived but most have been lost, irretrievably lost. Unlike bison and forests, they cannot be revived. The moral of the tale stands as a corrective to the lore of journalists: nothing is more dead than yesterday's newspaper, except yesterday's destroyed newspaper.

CHAPTER 9

The Importance of
Being Bibliographical

WHY IS BIBLIOGRAPHY important? If it is to be more than a list of titles, what use is it? The question has acquired new pertinence now that texts have become both more available and less trustworthy, thanks to the Internet. Students usually download texts from computers without asking where they came from, and they frequently get garbage. But the problem is not new.

Here is a passage from the first printed version of *King Lear* (the quarto edition of 1608, III. iv. 118): "swithald footed thrice the old a nellthu night more and her nine fold bid her, O light and her troth plight and arint thee, with arint thee."* It is

---

*F. P. Wilson, *Shakespeare and the New Bibliography,* Helen Gardner, ed. (Oxford, 1970), p. 121. In the First Folio, the passage reads: "Swithold footed thrice the wold,/ He met the nightmare and her ninefold;/ Bid her alight/ And her troth plight,/ And aroint thee, witch, aroint thee!" For commentary on the passage in which Edgar sings about a female demon, see Stephen Orgel and A. R. Braunmuller, eds. *The Complete Pelican Shakespeare* (Penguin, London and New York, 2002), p. 1533.

seventeenth-century garbage, which probably was almost as incomprehensible to seventeenth-century readers as it is to us. To make sense of it, textual editors have drawn on folklore, philology, paleography, the history of religion, and their own intuition. They have concluded that Shakespeare meant to evoke the notion of Saint Withold driving away a female demon and her brood during a tempestuous night. This kind of textual criticism, accompanied by commentary and variants in footnotes and appendices, is familiar to any reader of Shakespeare. What can bibliography contribute to it?

Consider another example of trash in Shakespeare, the quarto edition of *The Merchant of Venice* published in 1619. At I. iii. 65–6 Antonio asks Bassanio whether Shylock knows how much Antonio wants to borrow: "are you resolu'd, How much he would haue?" In the original edition of *The Merchant of Venice*, a quarto of 1600, the lines read: "is hee yet possest How much ye would?" Which to prefer? We cannot know what Shakespeare intended, because no manuscript of his plays survives—except perhaps three pages, written in his hand, from the unperformed tragedy of *Sir Thomas More*. But we can identify the most corrupt passages in the early printed versions.

By analysis of the physical copies, bibliographers have determined that the type of the 1619 quarto was set by the same compositor, a particularly slipshod workman whom they call Compositor B, who set nine other quartos of Shakespearean or pseudo-Shakespearean plays in the same year, using earlier editions as his copy. When he came upon a phrase that he considered deficient, he "improved" it. So the 1619 version of those lines is pure Compositor B, and the text of the play as a whole (it has an average of one significant error in every 23 lines) is very impure Shakespeare.

Moreover, B also composed about half the text of the First Folio, our main source for reconstructing Shakespeare's oeuvre. To make sense of Shakespeare, therefore, it is not enough to be a literary critic. One must also be a bibliographer—or at least understand enough of bibliography to know how books came into being in the late sixteenth and early seventeenth centuries.*

This kind of bibliography—usually called "descriptive" or "analytical" bibliography to distinguish it from the book-listing or "enumerative" variety—became a powerful force in the humanities during the first half of the twentieth century. But what exactly was it, and did it have implications for anything besides the editing of texts? Sir Walter Greg, the ultimate authority in these matters, defined bibliography as "the science of the material transmission of literary documents."** His formulation was contested by some who found "science" too positivistic and "literary" too narrow, since bibliographical analysis could be applied in principle to any kind of text and any form of communication. But the emphasis on materiality appealed to all bibliographers, because all of them studied books as physical objects. By learning how texts became imbedded in paper as typographical signs and transmitted to readers as pages bound in books, they hoped to understand a fundamental aspect of literature itself.

---

*For a discussion of this problem and of bibliography in general, see Philip Gaskell, *A New Introduction to Bibliography* (Clarendon Press, Oxford, 1972), pp. 336–360.

**Greg's definition, which probably was not meant to be an ex cathedra pronouncement about science, appeared in his article of 1912, "What Is Bibliography?" For a discussion of it, see G. Thomas Tanselle, "Bibliography and Science" in *Studies in Bibliography* vol. 27 (1974), p. 62.

Greg and R. B. McKerrow began to work out the basic concepts and techniques of this "new bibliography," as it came to be called, when they were students at Trinity College, Cambridge, in the 1890s. With the publication of *An Introduction to Bibliography for Literary Students* by McKerrow in 1928 and *Principles of Bibliographical Description* by Fredson Bowers in 1949, bibliography emerged as a coherent discipline with standards that had coalesced into an orthodoxy. By 1950, bibliography became a requirement in graduate programs for the PhD in many English departments. Along with philology and other professional skills, graduate students learned how to recognize formats, collate signatures, detect cancels, distinguish typefaces, trace watermarks, analyze artwork, and identify bindings.

Shakespearean studies especially flourished in this environment, because the early editions of the plays, published at a low point in the history of printing, are full of errors and cannot be corrected against an original manuscript. As far as we know, Shakespeare took no part in their publication. For him, it seems, the performance was what counted, and he probably modified the scripts as the action evolved on the stage. We can imagine his "foul papers" (early drafts) and prompt books, but to come up with texts we have to find a way through the faulty editions thrown together in the printing shops of his day. *Hamlet* appeared first in a primitive quarto of 1603, next in a quarto of 1604–5, which is twice as long, and then in the folio of 1623, which has 85 new lines and differs greatly from both of the earlier editions. *King Lear* presents so many puzzles that its most recent editors printed two versions of it. They are radically different, yet each conforms to the most exacting bibliographical standards and each may represent a version that Shakespeare considered at one point to be final. So we now have two *King Lears*, as well as older, conflated editions, and we are richer for it, thanks to bibliography.*

Textual conundrums of this sort inspired generations of scholars to feats of ever-greater virtuosity. By poring over early editions, they have traced typographical clues of every variety—inconsistent spelling, irregularities in spacing, chipped type, anything that could help them reconstruct the production processes of Elizabethan printing shops and therefore get closer to Shakespeare's missing copy. Many learned to set type themselves and turned into amateur letter-press printers. In their imaginations, PhDs became companions of the workers who first turned Shakespeare's words into books. It was an intoxicating idea, and it did not last.

Bibliography has not disappeared, but it has been pushed aside and ignored by more recent trends in literary scholarship. From the New Criticism of the 1940s to the deconstruction of the 1960s and the new historicism of the 1980s, the study of texts became increasingly detached from their embodiment in books. Bibliography began to look like an arcane discipline that might have uses for editing Shakespeare but little relevance for understanding modern literature. Some modern works, from *Pamela* to *Ulysses*, posed important bibliographical problems, but most could be edited with minimal notes about textual variants. In 1968 Edmund Wilson raised a storm by denouncing editions sponsored by the Modern Language Association for bibliographical overkill—he mentioned a project in which eighteen editorial workers were

---

*Stanley Wells and Gary Taylor, *The Complete Oxford Shakespeare* (Oxford University Press, Oxford, 1987), and Stephen Orgel and A. R. Braunmuller, eds., *The Complete Pelican Shakespeare* (Penguin, London and New York, 2002).

preparing an edition of *Tom Sawyer* by reading the text backward—and when the polemics died down, bibliography had lost much of its appeal. It disappeared from graduate programs and even from most library schools. To a generation that had witnessed the collapse of the canon and the rise of the Internet, fine-grained analysis of old books no longer was attractive.

In the midst of this self-questioning, the inevitable occurred: heresy. All orthodoxies generate heretics, but the Martin Luther of bibliography, Donald F. McKenzie, was especially threatening to the old guard, because he could beat the best of them at their own game. Having assimilated the Bowers principles and developed into an expert printer himself, McKenzie left his native New Zealand for Cambridge, England, where he wrote a PhD dissertation under Philip Gaskell, a master bibliographer. The book that resulted, *The Cambridge University Press, 1696–1712* (1966), was hailed as one of the most rigorous works ever written in the tradition of Greg and McKerrow. It had a disquieting aspect, however, because not only did McKenzie provide a bibliographical analysis of every book produced by the Cambridge University Press during those sixteen years, but he also related the physical evidence to manuscripts from the archives of the press, and the manuscripts revealed that things had not taken place as they should have, according to the conventional wisdom.

Compositors did not supply pressmen with formes (pages of type arranged inside an iron frame and locked in place so as to be ready for printing) in a consistent pattern. On the contrary, a compositor would send a completed forme to whatever press was free. So at one point or other, all the press-men of the shop often ran off copies of a particular book. Moreover, compositors also switched frequently from one job to another. They might set the type for one forme of a trea-tise like Newton's *Principia*, published by the CUP in 1713, then compose a bill of lading or a receipt, and later take up a book of sermons. Some tasks took longer than others and some were more urgent, so the foreman distributed them in the most efficient way, and several books were always mov-ing through production at the same time, each following its own, erratic rhythm. The regularity of output at the shop level compensated for the irregularities in the labor of each man, a way of organizing work that McKenzie called "concurrent production." It sounded innocent enough as an idea; but when he developed all its implications, he seemed to sap the foundations of orthodox bibliography.

Previous bibliographers had assumed that each book would move through the chain of production according to a consistent, linear pattern: a certain compositor would feed formes to the printers at a certain press, who would run off the edition, frequently leaving traces of their activity in the pattern of headlines at the top of the page, direction lines at the bottom, or press figures (usually numbers added at the bottom to identify the work of individual pressmen). It there-fore would be possible to construct a series of inferences, moving backwards through the production process from the physical copy, to a press, a compositor, and, at least to some extent, the original manuscript, even if it were missing, as in the case of Shakespeare. Above all, Shakespeare. The search for reliable texts of his plays drove the whole discipline.

The greatest Shakespearean bibliographers, notably Greg and Charlton Hinman, allowed for irregularities. The supreme study of a book from the era of Shakespeare, Hinman's *The Printing and Proof-Reading of the First Folio of Shakespeare* (1963), showed how the First Folio came into being, forme by forme, while other books were being printed at the same shop. At one point Hinman even used the term "concurrent production." But most bibliographers took the individual book rather than the output of the entire shop as the unit of analysis, and this line of reasoning, valid enough within its own limits, led them to string together questionable hypotheses about the men who produced the first printed copies of Shakespeare. In place of workers made of flesh and blood—preindustrial artisans who worked in erratic spurts and knocked off for bouts with the likes of Falstaff and Mistress Quickly—they substituted ghostly abstractions like Compositor B surrounded by A, C, and others, who were deemed to have turned out quartos and folios at regular rhythms in accordance with the principles of bibliographical science.

Not that these imaginary beings worked like robots. On the contrary, it seemed possible to demonstrate that one man had unusually erratic spelling, that another frequently mixed up homonyms, that a third worked from an inadequate font of type, and that all of them scattered idiosyncratic marks on the pages in patterns that revealed their hands at work as distinct from Shakespeare's. By identifying the passages that they mangled—in the case of Compositor B's *Merchant of Venice*, 40 words or phrases of his own that he substituted for Shakespeare's—bibliographers hoped to isolate the alien elements in the greatest works in the English language. It was a process of elimination, essentially negative in its findings, but it brought the modern reader closer to what Shakespeare had actually written.

If the printing shop operated according to the principle of concurrent production, however, it would be difficult to determine precise patterns of production; one could not link specific passages to specific compositors with complete confidence; and the chain of inferences could break at crucial points. A, B, C, and the rest might be figments of overheated bibliographical imaginations, mere "printers of the mind." That was the title McKenzie fixed to an essay of 1969, which shook the world of rare book rooms as if it were an earthquake. For the next decade scholars debated the principles of bibliography with all the passion that academics are capable of injecting into academic questions. They were generally ignored by the rest of the world, which had other things on its mind during those years. But to bibliographers, the stakes were enormous. McKenzie seemed to expose a seismic fault that ran right through their discipline.

The orthodox bibliographers defended their position with two arguments: first, that the Cambridge University Press, a small, specialized business in a provincial town at the beginning of the eighteenth century, could not be taken to typify operations in the larger printing shops of London nearly a hundred years earlier; second, that archival evidence did not invalidate the basic principle of using the analysis of books as physical objects to reach conclusions about the process of their printing—notably in the case of the early editions of Shakespeare, for that is what generated most of the heat in the polemics. If bibliography could not provide a reliable method for editing Shakespeare's texts, what good was it?

McKenzie dealt with the first argument by drawing on evidence from the papers of William Bowyer, a large London printer, which were discovered in 1963. They confirmed the principle of concurrent production and showed even more complex and irregular patterns in the flow of work, which was frequently shared by several shops as well as by several workmen. A few years later, Jacques Rychner demonstrated that McKenzie's analysis also held true for the production of books in the printing shop of the Société typographique de Neuchâtel in Switzerland. To be sure, the archives in Cambridge, London, and Neuchâtel all came from the eighteenth century. But there were no significant changes in the technology of printing from 1500 (or perhaps even in Gutenberg's time) to 1800. All three manuscript sources—and additional documentation from two other eighteenth-century London printers, William Strahan and Charles Ackers—proved that McKenzie was right: production in early-modern printing shops did not follow the regular pattern ascribed to it by orthodox bibliography.

But could manuscript material from the eighteenth century disprove arguments based on the physical analysis of Shakespearean quartos and folios? McKenzie never went that far. In fact, he produced the most thorough account of how Compositor B botched *The Merchant of Venice*. There was nothing wrong in principle with ascribing particular passages to compositors who could be called A or B or anything else. We even know a little bit about the actual men who worked in William Jaggard's printing shop where the First Folio was produced in 1622–23—including the fact that a John Shakespeare, apparently no relation to William, had served as an apprentice to Jaggard from 1610 to 1617. By minute study of the Folio, quire by quire, Hinman thought he had found a way to identify the compositors behind the text and thus get " . . . a little closer to the truth of what Shakespeare wrote."*

---

*Charlton Hinman, *The Printing and Proof-Reading of the First Folio of Shakespeare* (Oxford at the Clarendon Press, Oxford, 1963), I, p. vii.

Forty years after he published *The Printing and Proof-Reading of the First Folio of Shakespeare*, it seems that he, too, was right. The latest study of the Folio, by Peter Blayney, a partisan of McKenzie, has confirmed nearly all of Hinman's conclusions. Blayney has identified a few more compositors and modified Hinman's account of proof-reading. It now appears that the actors from Shakespeare's troupe had corrected the proof before the compositors added stop-press corrections during the printing. The first edition included three distinct issues: one had thirty-five plays; one had thirty-six, including *Troilus and Cressida* but without its prologue; and one had thirty-six with *Troilus*, prologue and all. The printers scattered clues to these irregularities by marks left in the text. In some cases they crossed out a redundant page of *Romeo and Juliet*. In others, they left in corrections added by hand during the final proof-reading. The text was always changing, always slipping morphologically from one state to another.

———

That lesson, from "the most important single book in English literature," as Helen Gardner put it,* bore on a larger issue raised by McKenzie's apparent heresies: bibliography might help resolve some difficulties peculiar to the editing of Shakespeare, but what could it contribute to the general understanding of literature? McKenzie himself addressed this problem in an essay of 1977, "Typography and Meaning: The Case of William Congreve," which proved to be almost as influential as "Printers of the Mind."

———

Shakespeare and the New Bibliography, p. x.

Congreve made a particularly interesting case to study, because he straddled two typographical eras. The first editions of his plays, casually printed quartos from the 1690s, were nearly as crude as the quartos of Shakespeare, whereas the three-volume, octavo edition of his works in 1710 exuded the stateliness of a classic. Which to prefer, the seventeenth- or the eighteenth-century Congreve? McKenzie faced this choice in preparing a critical edition of the works. He began by rejecting Greg's famous distinction between "substantives," or the basic text of a play, and "accidentals," typographical ingredients such as ornaments or extra spacing added by the printer to separate the scenes of a play. To Greg, accidentals were merely a matter of presentation, not one that affected the meaning of a text. To McKenzie, they were crucial in mediating the difference between two kinds of experience: watching a performance on a stage as opposed to reading a text on a page. Whatever effects the playwright originally had in mind when he composed a script, his play took on new meaning when it became a book, because at that point the dramatic action could only be imagined by readers working from typographical clues.

Congreve participated consciously in the shift from one medium to another, because by 1710 he had stopped writing for the stage and was concentrating on the publication of his plays. The octavo edition of his works set a standard for the new form of the book that came to prevail in the eighteenth century. Unlike the cumbersome folios and slap-dash quartos of the earlier era, it was small enough to be held comfortably in the hand and elegant enough to appeal to the tastes of a new consumer society. Congreve purged some of the bawdiest passages, but he retained most of the original texts. What gave them new meaning was the design of the book, a collaborative project worked out by Congreve with his close friend and publisher, Jacob Tonson, and Tonson's highly skilled printer, John Watts.

Using larger sheets (but smaller pages, because an octavo sheet was folded three times and a quarto twice before being assembled into a volume) and more balanced spacing, they gave the book a refined symmetry. In place of the minimal directions of the old quartos—usually nothing more than an "enter" or "exit" to signal new scenes—they set off scenes by numbers, typographical ornaments, and lists of characters. The reader could therefore imagine who was on stage at any given time and could see how all the parts fit within the whole. Scenes, plays, the entire oeuvre were clearly articulated, as in neoclassical architecture. Congreve took his place next to Shakespeare—who had appeared in similar typographical dress a year earlier—in what was beginning to emerge as a canon of classics.

At this point, McKenzie's argument converged with themes that had been developed in an adjoining field of research, the history of books. Unlike bibliographers, book historians studied all aspects in the production and diffusion of the printed word, including its connections with political and social change. For them, 1710 stood out as a turning point in the history of copyright. It was the year when Parliament passed the first copyright law entitled "A Bill for the Encouragement of Learning by Vesting the Copies of Printed books in the Authors, or Purchasers, of such Copies, during the Times therein Mentioned." As its title indicated, the law gave authors a new prominence. Although it did not actually mention them in its text, it recognized their proprietary right to the product of their imaginations. Alexander Pope showed that authors could support themselves from the sale of those rights. By mid-century

Samuel Johnson epitomized the professional writer, who lived from his pen instead of from patronage and gloried in his role of supplying demand on the literary market place. Literature itself was emerging as a semi-autonomous system organized around the printed book, in contrast to the world of letters from the sixteenth and seventeenth centuries. Under the Tudors and Stuarts, communication in the public sphere took place primarily through performances—on stage, from pulpits, at court, and in the streets. In Georgian England the printed word predominated, even though manuscript books continued to flourish (if published at less than 100 copies, a book could be produced more economically by scribes than by printers) and news still spread by word of mouth.

The publication of Congreve therefore belonged to a general process, the transformation of letters into literature, and McKenzie announced that it needed to be understood from a broad perspective, what he termed "the sociology of texts." From science to sociology, nothing could be further from the discipline of Greg and McKerrow; but it opened a way for Anglo-American bibliography to make a juncture with French "histoire du livre," the wide-ranging variety of book history developed by Lucien Febvre and Henri-Jean Martin. In *L'Apparition du livre* (1958), they related the impact of Gutenberg's invention to long-term social and economic phenomena such as the organization of scriptoria, the price of rags and parchment, and the development of trade routes. They stressed the need for quantitative evidence in order to measure continuity against change. And as partisans of the *Annales* school of history, they detected long-lasting patterns of structural stability, which led them to challenge accepted wisdom, including the belief that Gutenberg produced an immediate revolution in the publishing industry.

McKenzie attempted something similar by shifting from fine-grained analysis of individual books to the study of the London book trade as a whole, which he surveyed by making sweeps through all the surviving evidence from three years: 1644, 1668, and 1689. Research on this scale required a prodigious amount of labor, because McKenzie combined quantification from his main source, D. G. Wing's short-title catalogue of books printed between 1641 and 1700, with the examination of every copy that he could locate in major research libraries. By counting the number of sheets in each copy, he was able to make a better estimate of total output than by simply counting titles, and he could look at the entire literary landscape from the perspective of productivity and economics.

For 1668, Wing and a few additional sources provided a total of 491 titles, of which McKenzie physically studied 458. He could not produce a full analytical description of each of them, but his expert eye detected all sorts of trends and oddities. The names of the printers did not appear on more than half the title pages. Reprints accounted for nearly a third of the total output. And only 52 books bore some form of license or official permission to publish, despite the requirements of the Licensing Act of 1662. The booksellers' main concern was to protect their copyrights, and this they could do by informal "combinations" among themselves, such as joint arrangements for marketing and sales. It looked as if printers and booksellers went about their business without paying much attention to politics and without developing much of an appetite for innovation.

Conservative, commercial interests even dominated the trade during revolutionary times. By surveying nearly everything published in 1644 at the height of the English Civil War,

McKenzie found a surprising degree of continuity in overall production. He rejected the argument advanced by Christopher Hill and Keith Thomas that an unprecedented explosion of political literature took place in the early 1640s as a result of the freedom of the press. Neither the end of state control in 1641 nor the restoration of it in 1643 had much effect on the book trade, McKenzie argued, because booksellers continued to pursue profits in familiar ways without concern for changes in the law. Even Milton's *Areopagitica*, commonly celebrated as a manifesto for a free press, was not a protest against the licensing act of 1643 but rather a response to harassment concerning his divorce tracts.

When the revolution of 1688 produced another change in the rules of the game and prepublication censorship ended in 1695, McKenzie again saw the prevalence of continuity and economic interests rather than the triumph of liberty. The Stationers' Company lost its monopoly of the book trade, but its members continued to dominate the business through combinations known as "congers." Even authors remained oblivious to changes in the political climate when it came to appearing openly before the public by putting their names on title pages. Only 40 percent of the titles carried the author's name in 1644 and only 43 percent in 1668. In England as in France, quantification led to revisionist results: long-term socio-economic trends seemed more important than momentary shifts in politics.

———

McKenzie was the only bibliographer who could challenge accepted views by working in two registers, enumerative as well as analytical bibliography. But he did not have the last word. He would not have wanted to. Two books published after his death in March 1999 provide a measure of what he had accomplished and of what his work opened up for others to continue. The first, *Making Meaning. "Printers of the Mind" and Other Essays*, edited by two of his former students, Peter D. McDonald and Michael F. Suarez, S. J., gathers his most important essays in a single volume, arranged artfully by theme and introduced in a way that brings out their originality. They show McKenzie's mind at work, undoing *idées fixes* and extracting new ideas from the most intractable material. They also raise the issue of bibliography's importance beyond the field of textual criticism, where it originated.

The second work, *Books & Bibliography: Essays in Commemoration of Don McKenzie*, shows how that issue has been addressed by the latest generation of bibliographers and book historians. In it, they chase hares set loose by McKenzie over the last thirty years. They pursue the study of book production deep into the printing shops of the nineteenth century, analyze the interplay of oral and printed means of communication, and investigate the transmission of "texts" in the broadest sense of the term—in music, photography, and architecture. McKenzie taught that bibliography can go beyond books. By following his leads, his successors have shown that it offers a way to understand the reproduction of cultural forms of all kinds, provided that they lend themselves to rigorous description.

Meanwhile, book historians have continued to penetrate more of the mysteries that go back to Gutenberg. In 2000, when they celebrated the six hundredth anniversary of his birth—his putative birth in 1400: we know much less about him than the little we know about Shakespeare—a burst of publications attested to the vitality of bibliographical scholarship. By new techniques of analyzing paper, ink, and type, experts such as Paul Needham, Richard Schwab, and Blaise Agüera y Arcas have transformed our knowledge of how the first printed books were produced. In 1991, the Folger Library produced an exhibition of its treasures, and Peter Blayney explained them in a short book, *The First Folio of Shakespeare*, which synthesized the most advanced Shakespearean scholarship in language that could be understood by any layman. Bibliography, he showed, had not run out of energy, and it could speak to the general public.

It seems clear in retrospect that the boundary disputes of the 1970s did not damage the discipline and that bibliographers have everything to gain by joining book historians in collaborative efforts to break through boundaries. The problems to be solved today extend far beyond the texts of Shakespeare. They appear in communication systems of all varieties, including the Internet, where digitized texts are detached from their moorings in printed books, and e-mail messages leave trails that can easily evaporate. Those were the kinds of problems that fascinated Don McKenzie when he died, too young, in 1999. He did not undermine bibliography, far from it. His heresies have given it new life.

CHAPTER 10

The Mysteries of Reading

Tᴉᴍᴇ ᴡᴀs ᴡʜᴇɴ ʀᴇᴀᴅᴇʀs kept commonplace books. Whenever they came across a pithy passage, they copied it into a notebook under an appropriate heading, adding observations made in the course of daily life. Erasmus instructed them how to do it; and if they did not have access to his popular *De Copia*, they consulted printed models or the local schoolmaster. The practice spread everywhere in early modern England, among ordinary readers as well as famous writers like Francis Bacon, Ben Jonson, John Milton, and John Locke. It involved a special way of taking in the printed word. Unlike modern readers, who follow the flow of a narrative from beginning to end (unless they are digital natives and click through texts on machines), early modern Englishmen read in fits and starts and jumped from book to book. They broke texts into fragments and assembled them into new patterns by transcribing them in different sections of their notebooks.

Then they reread the copies and rearranged the patterns while adding more excerpts. Reading and writing were therefore inseparable activities. They belonged to a continuous effort to make sense of things, for the world was full of signs: you could read your way through it; and by keeping an account of your readings, you made a book of your own, one stamped with your personality.

The era of the commonplace book reached its peak in the late Renaissance, although commonplacing as a practice probably began in the twelfth century and remained widespread among the Victorians. It disappeared long before the advent of the sound bite. Yet it still survives in places. The best example of a twentieth-century commonplace book is *Geoffrey Madan's Notebooks*, published by the Oxford University Press in 1981. Perhaps it is the last of the line, for it has fallen out of print and seems to have been forgotten, except in some senior common rooms of British universities. But it deserves to be rescued from oblivion, because it is a great read, especially for anyone interested in reading itself as a way of making sense of the world.

Educated at Eton and Oxford, Madan survived injury in World War I but came down with meningitis in 1924 and spent the rest of his life in retirement, living off a private income and observing the human comedy from the clubs of London and the high tables of Oxford. When he recorded his observations, he adhered to the Erasmian principle of distilling things down to their essence and entering them in notebooks, as if he were storing rare wine to be served for *dégustation* in future conversations. As Erasmus advised, Madan devised his own set of rubrics for classifying his material. But the rubrics corresponded to the world of a man about town in the 1920s and 1930s rather than a Christian humanist from the sixteenth century. "Viniana," for example, was devoted to wine itself, one of Madan's three main passions, the others being old silver and rare books:

> Queen Victoria "strengthening" claret with whisky.
> —Gladstone, letter to Mrs. Gladstone, 1864

> I see you have been brought up in the best school,—the school of port: and if you will take an old man's advice, Sir, always drink it out of a claret-glass.
> —The Revd. F. Bertie, to Lord Ernle at All Souls

> "Only half-full, thank you." Shy woman, with Savoy brandy-glass.

Madan's taste in anecdotes ran to the incongruous, which he listed in lapidary fashion under "Humorous and Memorable":

> Instead of being arrested, as we stated, for kicking his wife down a flight of stairs and hurling a lighted kerosene lamp after her, the Revd. James P. Wellman died unmarried four years ago.
> —From an American newspaper,
> quoted by Burne-Jones in a letter to Lady Horner

> Omlet, Omlet, dies is dein Feyder's spooke.
> —Dutch *Hamlet*

> *Important if true.* Inscription which Kinglake wanted on all churches.

"Academica" provided a rubric for inside jokes, delivered straight, with an Eton-Oxford accent:

H. M. Butler: "Christ, in a very real sense, a Trinity man."

What sort of place *is* it, sir? Something in the Keble line?
—Raymond Asquith's scout
on his return from Cambridge

Hornby [Headmaster of Eton]: "I rather wish Shelley had been at Harrow."

"Beauty, Point, and Charm" included Madan's own observations along with those of others who knew how to pick out the revealing detail or the arresting turn of phrase:

Note in Gladstone's Dante (which I saw at the Rosebery sale) on "*Nel mezzo del cammin . . .*": 15–49 [years old].

Odd that we call the end of a rope or a chain, the *end*; while in Greek it is the *beginning*.

Peel's smile: like the silver plate on a coffin.
—O'Connell

Madan's humor combined snobbery with patrician self-parody, the kind that reinforces social distinctions while making fun of them:

Trousers should shiver on the shoe but not break.
—Arnold Bennett's tailor

A gentleman: superficially perhaps, a man who never looks as if he'd just had his hair cut.

No gentleman can be without three copies of a book; one for show (and this he will probably keep at his country house), another for use, and a third at the service of his friends.

—Richard Heber

But his humor had an edge to it, because after the slaughter of World War I, everything looked absurd, including patriotism and religion:

We shelled the Turks from 9 to 11: and then, it being Sunday, had Divine Service.

—Commander, R.N., to Admiralty (1915)

I never read poetry. It might soften me.

—General Hindenburg (1912)

Duke of Wellington disapproved of soldiers cheering, as too nearly an expression of opinion.

Queen Victoria "indicating with uplifted fan" that a sermon should stop.

—*Quarterly Review*, April 1901

The citations and bons mots flow by endlessly; but instead of giving the impression of disordered jottings, they convey a coherent view of the world, one both intensely personal and shot through with the flavor of its time. Madan's commonplace book blends Edwardian preciosity with post-war disabusement, and it does so without explanation or exposition, merely by juxtaposing remarks culled from reading and conversation.

———

Why pause over this arcane, forgotten book? Because it shows how an archaic genre could be used to impose order on experience in modern times. Commonplace books served far more effectively in this manner several centuries earlier, when they were standard tools of readers. By studying them, historians and literary scholars have come closer to understanding reading, both as a specific cultural practice and as a general way of construing the world. But it is a tricky business, especially when the researcher moves from questions about who readers were and what they read to the problems of how they made sense of books.

Thomas Jefferson is a case in point. When his commonplace book first was published in 1928, its editor, Gilbert Chinard, celebrated it as a key that would unlock Jefferson's impenetrable personality as well as his view of the world. That world view came to epitomize the American Enlightenment, but it looked odd as a set of excerpts from Jefferson's reading as a young man. From the age of about 15 to 30, he copied the excerpts on folded sheets of foolscap paper. Sometime in his mid-thirties, he sorted out the sheets that he wanted to keep and had them bound in a volume of 123 leaves, which he consulted and quoted for the rest of his life, though he did not add any more passages to it.

It is a "literary" commonplace book, as opposed to the "legal" commonplace book that he used for his work as a lawyer. Of its 407 entries, 339 are citations of poetry, including 14 from Ossian, the pseudo-Celtic bard invented by James Macpherson and considered by Jefferson to be "the greatest poet that has ever existed." Jefferson had a low opinion of novels and cited only one, *Tristram Shandy*. He preferred the standard fare of the classics that he studied as a schoolboy under the Rev. James Maury and as a student at the College of William and Mary: Homer, Euripides, Horace, Virgil, and Ovid—but not Plato, whom he scorned. His Cicero was the somber moralist of the *Tusculan Disputations* rather than the orator. His British poets included contemporary favorites like Edward Young and James Thomson along with Shakespeare, Milton, and Pope. But his selections from the poetry were less predictable than his choice of poets. For example, he treated Samuel Butler's mock heroic *Hudibras* as a source of solemn moralizing, unlike other Virginians, who used it to poke fun at Yankee puritanism. In fact, he did not betray the slightest sense of humor anywhere in his commonplace book. Nothing could be further from the world of Geoffrey Madan, though Madan was a more accomplished classicist.

"The lost world of Thomas Jefferson," as Daniel Boorstin called it, was a serious place, saturated with Enlightenment philosophy; but few philosophers appeared in the commonplace book, perhaps because Jefferson used it primarily as a record of his favorite readings in the classics and belles-lettres. The exception is Henry Saint-John, Viscount Bolingbroke, who accounts for forty percent of all the material that Jefferson selected for the final version, which he had bound in the 1780s. He admired Bolingbroke as a bold commentator on the Bible and copied passages such as the following, which is quoted as Jefferson copied it: "now there are gross

defects, [a]nd palpable falsehoods, in almost every page of
the [s]criptures, and the whole tenor of them is such as no
man who acknowledges a supreme all-perfect being [c]an
beleive to be his word." Bolingbroke was the source of Jefferson's famous advice to his nephew, Peter Carr: "Fix reason firmly in her seat, and call to her tribunal every fact, every opinion. . . . Read the Bible then, as you would read Livy or Tacitus."

That may sound reassuringly familiar: the Founding Father was a secular rationalist as a young bachelor. But what is one to make of the passages Jefferson selected from Milton, such as Adam's lament in *Paradise Lost*?

> . . . *all but a Rib,*
> *Crooked by Nature, bent (as now appears)*
> *More to the Part sinister from me drawn;*
> *Well if thrown out, as supernumerary*
> *To my just Number found!—O! Why did God[,]*
> *Creator wise! that Peopl'd highest Heav'n*
> *With Spirits masculine, create at last*
> *This Novelty on Earth, this fair Defect*
> *Of Nature? And not fill the World at once*
> *With Men, as Angels, without feminine?*
> *Or find some other Way to generate*
> *Mankind? This Mischeif had not then befall['n]*
> *And more that shal befal: innumerable*
> *Disturbances on Earth through female Snares,*
> *And straight Conjunction with this Sex!*

Why did young Jefferson select that passage, one of the most infamous in the annals of misogyny? And why did he choose an equally damning selection from *Samson Agonistes*?

Therefore God's universal Law
Gave to Man despotic Power
Over his Female in due Awe,
Nor from that Right to part an Hour,
Smile she or lour:
So shall he least Confusion draw
On his whole Life, no sway'd
By female Usurpation, or dismay'd.

Douglas Wilson, who produced the most recent and most scholarly edition of the commonplace book, has an answer. Jefferson copied out these passages and others that are equally unsettling—angry descriptions of rebellion, morbid accounts of death—during a period of emotional turmoil. He made his first excerpts soon after his father's death, when he was 14, and the next ones as an adolescent, when he had difficulty adjusting to his mother's rule over the household. The hostile references to women coincided with his prolonged bachelorhood, and they came to an end with his happy marriage to Martha Wayles Skelton in 1772. Jefferson's commonplacing ended at about the same time. Having committed himself to a career as a lawyer and a politician, he stopped reading poetry and closed the book on his earlier emotions, although he opened it, consulted it, and quoted it at various times for the rest of his life.

This interpretation will not do for Kenneth Lockridge. In a fascinatingly original and iconoclastic monograph published in 1992, he treated Jefferson's commonplace book as one of two great manifestoes of misogyny from eighteenth-century Virginia. The other was the commonplace book of William Byrd II, a collection of anecdotes about voracious females and inadequate males, interspersed with sexual folklore. For example:

Popilia being askt by a very curious Person of her own Sex, why Brutes woud never admit the male after they had once conceivd? answered with the true Spirit of a woman, because they are Brutes, and know no better.

Barren women are commonly more lascivious than fruitfull ones, because [of] the Heat of the womb, which is often the cause of Sterility, & at the same time the fomenter of wantoness.

To rub the Penis with oyl of Lavender is of great use to procure Erection: but the drink usd in Provence calld Sambajeu, is much better for that purpose; which is compounded of Wine, yold of Eggs, Saffran, Sugar, & mace, which may be boild together, or else drunk raw with glorious Success.

Byrd makes an easy target. As Lockridge describes him, he was a nasty piece of work: an impotent patriarch, who vented his sexual, social, and political failures in rage against women. But Thomas Jefferson? He carried "patriarchal rage" even further, according to Lockridge. True, Jefferson did not accompany the citations in his commonplace book with comments of his own. But by selecting the most egregiously hostile remarks on women from the endless variety of literature available to him, he injected so much fear and loathing in his picture of the war between the sexes that, as Lockridge sees it, he expressed a pathological strain of "gendering" in his psyche and his culture.

To support this argument, Lockridge cites Jefferson's supposedly difficult relations with his mother, who took over the patriarchal estate after the death of his father. He claims that

Jefferson chose an especially submissive mate in Martha Wayles and avoided emotional engagement with women after her death. Instead of remarrying, he redesigned Monticello as "a single man's pavilion of himself," suppressing space for family. And insofar as he made room for family life, it took the form of paternal imperatives, which revealed his underlying anxieties. Thus his admonition about cleanliness to his eleven-year-old daughter Martha: "Some ladies think they may under the privileges of the dishabille be loose and negligent of their dress in the morning. But be you from the moment you rise till you go to bed as cleanly and properly dressed as at the hours of dinner or tea."

As evidence goes, it is pretty circumstantial; and we have been there before, in a long run of psycho-biographies that pretend to penetrate the souls of the dead by reading domestic details as if they were tea leaves. Most scholars probably will prefer harder facts, like the evidence from DNA that linked Jefferson to Sally Hemings—who does not figure in Lockridge's argument, although she could fit into it. But Lockridge's reading of Jefferson's commonplace book challenges conventional wisdom in a compelling way. He treats it like a Rorschach test, and invokes Foucault rather than Freud. The bits and pieces of literature that Jefferson assembled are therefore deemed to operate like an epistemological field: the relations among them and spaces between them suggest an unconscious process of ordering. The horror of female sexuality conjugates into fear of male inadequacy, anxiety over patriarchy, horror at disorder, and obsession with death.

In order to do justice to the argument, one must read all the entries in the commonplace book with an eye to the underlying affinities that hold it together as a whole. Lockridge does detect a pattern, even if he cannot accommodate

exceptions to it, such as this passage from Thomas Otway's
Venice Preserved:

> *Can there in Women be such glorious Faith?*
> *Sure all ill Stories of thy Sex are false!*
> *O Woman! lovely Woman! Nature made thee*
> *To temper Man: we had been Brutes without you:*
> *Angels are painted fair to look like you:*
> *There's in you all that we beleive of Heav'n,*
> *Amazing Brightness, Purity & Truth,*
> *Eternal joy, & everlasting Love.*

Whether or not one accepts Lockridge's conclusions, he
showed that the lost world of Thomas Jefferson was not the
happy, rational order imagined by Jefferson's earlier biographers. And more important, he demonstrated the possibility
of studying commonplace books as cosmologies.

For a still more thorough study and a richer run of commonplacing, one can turn to Kevin Sharpe's new book on
William Drake, a voracious reader and bit player in the conflicts that convulsed England from 1640 to 1660. Nothing set
Drake apart from the other country squires of his time, except his love of books. He received a conventional education
at Oxford, studied law for a while in London, managed an
estate in Buckinghamshire, and got himself elected to Parliament in 1640.

Like many MPs, Drake avoided taking sides as England
slid into civil war. In 1641, he published a speech that advo-
cated both frequent parliaments and a strong executive power.

In 1642, he subscribed L. 200 for the maintenance of horse in the forces both of Parliament and the Crown. In 1643, while battles raged, he left for the Continent and stayed there, except for some brief trips back to England, until the Restoration. He took up his seat in Parliament as a supporter of Charles II in 1660 and kept it until his death in 1669. He was a survivor rather than a man of action, an observer who watched politics from a safe distance, a backbencher who remained in the background.

Although Drake did not participate in the great events of the mid-century, he followed them closely through the press and spliced the information that he culled from pamphlets and broadsides with excerpts from wide-ranging reading in history and philosophy. All of it went into commonplace books: fifteen from about 1627 to the mid-1640s and twenty-two from the mid-1640s through the 1650s. A further seventeen volumes contain miscellaneous notes and letters. They can be supplemented by a one-volume political diary, which contains entries from 1631 to 1642, and books from Drake's library, which have extensive annotations. Taken together, these sources provide the richest cache of material about a reader and his reading anywhere in existence.

Unfortunately, however, Drake rarely commented on events, probably because he did not want to compromise himself. His diary is a disappointment for anyone who wants to follow a backbencher's reactions to a revolution, and the entries in his commonplace books cannot be dated with precision. They do, however, show how he understood reading and made use of it. Some examples:

The meat which we have taken, so long as it swimmeth whole in our stomachs, is a burden, but when it changeth from that which it was, then at length it turns into strength and nourishment. The same let us do in our reading books. Let us not suffer these things to remain entire which we have gathered from various authors for they will not then be ours, but let us endeavor to digest and concoct them— otherwise they will fill the memory and leave the understanding void and empty.

Be sure not to study much books of learning for they divert business, take up the memory too much and keep one from more useful things.

For the gaining wisdom there is nothing more effectual than frequent reading, apothegms, proverbs, prudent fables, wisest speeches . . . emblems, strategems, judgements and sentences raised upon various occasions in history.

Drake understood reading as digestion, a process of extracting the essence from books and of incorporating them into himself. He favored bite-sized bits of text, which could be useful in their application to everyday life. For reading should not be aimed at erudition; it should help a man get ahead in the world, and its most helpful chunks came in the form of proverbs, fables, and even the mottoes written into emblem books.

Reading of this sort belonged to a mental universe far removed from ours, even though we, too, may read for utilitarian purposes. The alien quality of Drake's mentality stands out in the examples of proverbial wisdom that he copied into his commonplace books:

Choose a horse made and a wife to make.

A man should never commend his wife, wine or horse, for it tempts borrowing.

Dissimulation is no less profitable . . . than preservatives in physic.

As a man is befriended so his cause is ended.

Of course, proverbs can be interpreted in a hundred different ways, and there is no obvious way to fit the hundreds of citations in Drake's commonplace books into one, unifying interpretation. But help can be had from a study of some similar material by Lisa Jardine and Anthony Grafton.* They published a dazzlingly original analysis of marginalia by Gabriel Harvey, a lawyer and secretary to the Earl of Leicester in Elizabethan England. Harvey read and reread a 1555 edition of Livy's *History of Rome* over a period of 22 years, leaving behind a trail of annotations, which often can be linked to contemporary events. In fact, he filled the margins with so many allusions and cross-references that they turned into a kind of palimpsest or a commonplace book within a book. They showed that Harvey never read his Livy straight through or by itself. Instead, he selected passages appropriate to the exigencies of the moment and assembled them, with excerpts from other classics, to be used as ammunition in rhetorical battles or advice to potential patrons. The actual combat took place above his head, in diplomatic missions or power plays at court. Harvey merely functioned as a munitions man, hoping that one

---

*Lisa Jardine and Anthony Grafton, "'Studied for Action': How Gabriel Harvey Read his Livy," *Past & Present*, no. 129 (November 1990), 31–78.

of his patrons would score a hit and reward him with a promotion. Classical culture belonged to the rough and tumble of Tudor-Stuart politics, and Harvey read his way through it, not in order to refine his knowledge but to get ahead in life.

When Kevin Sharpe set out to find the underlying logic to Drake's commonplace books, he detected the same classical-political culture that Grafton and Jardine had found between the lines and around the margins of Harvey's Livy. Drake and Harvey drew on the same sources and slanted them in the same direction: toward action rather than contemplation, for secular success instead of other-worldly wisdom. This ethos showed through glosses and cross-references. Like Harvey, Drake constantly cited Livy. He also cited Machiavelli and Machiavelli's citations of Livy. Then he rearranged the citations, added other authors, and worked in allusions to recent as well as ancient history. From Latin to Italian to English, from ancient Rome to Renaissance Florence to Stuart England, everything was refracted in everything else; yet it held together as a view of the world, thanks to an ordering principle: an improvised, amateur Machiavellianism.

Drake cited Machiavelli more often than any other author, but he did not respond to the patriotic, republican aspects of Machiavelli's writings. He merely culled through them for adages that might be useful in his efforts to improve his own lot in life while the Stuart monarchy disintegrated around him. The most striking quality of this selection process was its secularism. While his countrymen were killing themselves over disputes about the Book of Common Prayer, the legitimacy of bishops, and the meaning of the sacraments, Drake saw only power struggles. Never did he indicate the slightest sympathy for the conventional notion that England was and ought to be a Christian commonwealth. He worried about abuses of the royal prerogative in the 1630s and the need to reinforce it after 1642, but he did not mention the spiritual ingredient in the king's authority. He even interpreted the Bible as a collection of cautionary tales about whose ox might be gored, and he cross-referenced passages from the Gospels with excerpts from Machiavelli and Guicciardini, one more secular than the other.

When Drake came upon themes like love and friendship, he glossed them in an equally cynical spirit:

Love doth often much mischief in human life.

Never make thyself too inwardly familiar with any, and though thou mightest have less joy thou shall be sure to have less sorrow.

He outdid Jefferson in his negative view of women:

The woman is an imperfect creature . . . a creature ungovernable, unfaithful, changeable, cruel, and the slave to a thousand passions.

Our marriage bed often proves suddenly our death bed.

Whether or not Drake really expected eros to be swallowed up in thanatos, he never married. He eagerly awaited his father's death, when he expected to inherit the family estate; and he seems to have got on badly with his relatives. In social life, he did his best to disguise his feelings and to avoid intimate friendships. He saw little else than cunning and deceit in the world around him: every man pursued self-interest, no matter how loudly he proclaimed his allegiance to causes.

Life was a war of all against all; politics, the rule of the strong; history, a cyclical movement in and out of chaos:

There is a secret, intestine war between man and man.

The stronger gives what law he likes to the weaker.

All things dissolve and fall back into anarchy and confusion.

The cynicism runs so deep that Drake seems to have compounded Machiavelli with Hobbes.

That is Kevin Sharpe's interpretation. He pursues it with unflagging energy, through hundreds of pages of sibylline citations, across widely scattered manuscript sources, from histories to fables to proverbs to emblem books, and back again in a dizzying hermeneutic circle. It is a tour de force, but is it true?

As Sharpe sees it, "Drake out-machiavels even Old Nick" and made himself into a Hobbesian before he read Hobbes. But that raises a problem, because Drake merely cobbled together quotations, while Machiavelli and Hobbes wrote systematic treatises. Hobbes grounded his political theory in a carefully constructed materialist philosophy. And Machiavelli did not merely treat politics as a power game: he saw principles at work in power struggles, above all *virtù*—that is, patriotic virtue like the civic spirit that he hoped would save the Florentine republic. In contrast, Drake's collection of cynical proverbs and secular aphorisms seem to represent nothing more than a disenchanted attitude toward politics as power struggles.

Nonetheless, Sharpe insists that Drake "devised an intellectual system"—a "fully Machiavellian theory" built with solidly Hobbesian material, which recast politics as part of a "new intellectual and political culture." Drake forged a new sense of the self, in fact, a whole new world view, which transformed the mental landscape of early modern England, even though he never expounded any ideas of his own. How did he turn this trick? By reading. According to Sharpe, Drake's journey through books can be equated with England's passage through the seventeenth century.

Extravagant as it is, the argument deserves to be taken seriously. Drake read critically, excerpting passages and splicing them together in patterns that expressed an intensely personal outlook on the world. He read without regard for higher authority, either of Church or state, and in doing so he exercised his own judgment as an autonomous individual. His commonplace books bore the stamp of that consciousness. In a century of political and religious fervor, they expressed attitudes that would emerge a century later, in the age of Enlightenment: individualism, skepticism, secularism, utilitarianism, rationalism, and religious ideas bordering on deism.

Having immersed himself in Drake's reading, Sharpe can come up with plenty of evidence to connect that string of "isms" to a pattern of culture implicit in the commonplace books. But he disputes the notion of evidence itself. To him, it smells of positivism, a mode of historical argument that, he claims, has carried the study of British history into a dead end.

In order to make that charge stick, Sharpe begins his book with a discourse on method and a survey of historiography. He goes over the great debates that have divided historians of seventeenth-century Britain for the last fifty years, stressing the opposition between an "old guard" of social historians like Lawrence Stone and Christopher Hill, and "revisionists" like Conrad Russell and himself. As he sees it, the revisionists demolished the old-guard notion that the English Civil War was actually a revolution ignited by social conflict and ideological division. They demonstrated the contrary: the monarchy collapsed as an unintended consequence of internecine squabbles among a political elite who shared a fundamental consensus about politics and religion. However, having routed their elders and occupied the main terrain in the historiographical battles, the revisionists faced the problem of what to do next. An endlessly detailed account of political events would lead nowhere. But by following the lead of Sharpe, they can find the only way out of "post-revisionism"—namely, postmodernism, or a great leap into theory.

By theory, Sharpe means an amalgam of the work of Michel Foucault, Jacques Derrida, Jacques Lacan, Ferdinand de Saussure, Mikhail Bakhtin, Pierre Bourdieu, Roland Barthes, Hayden White, Clifford Geertz, Quentin Skinner, John Pocock, Hans Robert Jauss, Wolfgang Iser, Stanley Fish, Stephen Greenblatt, and the other usual suspects. They make up "a gallery of unknowns" to early modern historians, he claims—rather oddly, considering the saturation of references to them in scholarly journals over the last thirty years. Odder still is his notion that "theory" is a coherent whole, something that can be used to rescue historians shipwrecked on the shoals of positivism:

> My project is to suggest that for Renaissance scholars, for early modern historians, the issues and questions raised and some of the methods advocated by theory may help us to reimagine a Renaissance culture that did not share the positivism or "the organicist ideology of modernism. . . . "

It seems doubtful that by invoking "evidence" and "facts" the older generation subscribed to a mindless variety of positivism. And it seems unlikely that their successors can be

saved from future shipwrecks by means of self-reflective pro-
legomena about method and theory. Sharpe's triumphalist
version of historical debates and his claims to originality will
put off many readers. But that would be a pity, because he
has worked through a vast amount of unfamiliar material and
arrived at some challenging conclusions.

He is right, I think, to treat commonplace books as sites to
be mined for information about how people thought in a culture based on different assumptions from our own. By selecting and arranging snippets from a limitless stock of literature,
early modern Englishmen gave free play to a semi-conscious
process of ordering experience. The elective affinities that
bound their selections into patterns reveal an epistemology at
work below the surface. That kind of phenomenon does not
show up in conventional research and cannot be understood
without some recourse to theory. Foucault probably offers the
most helpful theoretical approach. His "archeology of knowledge" suggests a way to study texts as sites that bear the marks
of epistemological activity, and it has the advantage of doing
justice to the social dimension of thought.

That dimension can be at least surmised, thanks to other
studies of commonplace books and marginalia. Sharpe sur-
veys them all and extracts enough material to indicate some
underlying similarities in the reading practices of early modern Englishmen. They had all sorts of opinions and read all
sorts of books. But they read in the same way—segmentally,
by concentrating on small chunks of text and jumping from
book to book, rather than sequentially, as readers did a century later, when the rise of the novel encouraged the habit of
perusing books from cover to cover. Segmental reading compelled its practitioners to read actively, to exercise critical
judgment, and to impose their own pattern on their reading

matter. It was also adapted to "reading for action," an appropriate mode for men like Drake, Harvey, John Dee, John Rous, Sir Robert Cotton, Edward Hyde, and other contemporaries, who consulted books in order to get their bearings in perilous times, not to pursue knowledge for its own sake or to amuse themselves.

By mastering so much material and synthesizing it so aptly, Sharpe has made an important contribution to the history of reading. But he wants to do more—to demonstrate that the history of reading is the key to history in general, or at least to the seventeenth century. To Drake and his contemporaries, he insists, the mental sorting that went into commonplace books proved to be crucial in finding a way through the cutthroat politics of Renaissance courts. The result was a Machiavellian mentality—not that everyone in the educated elite adopted the same philosophy, but everyone tended to read the world in the same disabused manner.

They also turned their reading into writing, because commonplacing made them into authors. It forced them to write their own books; and by doing so they developed a still sharper sense of themselves as autonomous individuals. The authorial self took shape in the common man's commonplace book, not merely in the works of great writers. It belonged to the general tendency that Stephen Greenblatt has called "Renaissance self-fashioning."

Although that idea has nearly been worked to death among Renaissance scholars, Sharpe tries to breathe new life in it by applying it to politics. In setting out "to write himself," he argues, Drake "also wrote a script for society and state." Everyone who made marginal notes and compiled references "scripted a new political culture." At this point in the argument, the metaphors have to bear a good deal of strain.

Sharpe claims that Englishmen "were able to . . . constitute themselves as political agents" by reading, whether or not they read about state affairs; for politics was "a type of consciousness" and the psyche "a text of politics." "The Civil War itself became a contested text." So reading was everything: "We are what we read."

That may be better than the old slogan, proclaimed by the German Greens: "We are what we eat" (*"Man ist was man isst"*). But, again, is it true? Despite his mountain of notebooks and annotated volumes, Drake does not provide ideal material for a case study. He could not provide a close reading of English politics from 1643 to 1660, because he spent nearly all of that time abroad. Never does he mention the battles of the Civil War, the Putney debates, Pride's purge of Parliament, the trial and execution of Charles I, Cromwell's rise to power, the Commonwealth, Protectorate, or anything of importance during those momentous years. Instead of studying for action, he ran away from the action and shut himself up in his study. His notes about ancient Rome and Renaissance Florence may suggest concern about the spectacular events across the Channel, but were they really his? Only 15 of the 37 commonplace books were written in his hand. He might have dictated the others to a secretary, but the nature of his authorship, if it existed, remains a matter of conjecture. A great deal of guesswork also must go into the interpretation of the entries in his own hand, because none of them are dated. Unlike the notes of Harvey, they consist of endless excerpts, which cannot be connected with anything that was happening in the world of politics.

In attempting to answer that objection, Sharpe musters some evidence of the kind that he had rejected at the outset in his discourse on method. But ultimately he falls back on references to literary theory, as if they can do the job when the paper trail gives out in the archives. Sharpe's use of theory would carry more conviction if he did not proclaim it like a preacher. He harangues the reader, declaiming Derrida and brandishing Foucault. To those who have been through it all, it will sound suspiciously like Bible thumping.

If so, more's the pity, because at the heart of the book Sharpe demonstrates the existence of a Machiavellian style of reading that colored the political culture of early modern England. He does not prove that it was a philosophy, but he shows that it was a way of construing the world. This hardnosed, street-smart, seat-of-the-pants Machiavellianism, reinforced in places with vulgar, Hobbesian Realpolitik, probably spread from the courts of fifteenth-century Italy to the centralizing monarchies of France and Britain during the sixteenth and seventeenth centuries. By the time of Drake, Englishmen had learned to work through books in the same way that they negotiated through power systems. Their reading complemented their politics, even if it was not the same thing.

That point warrants pondering, because the history of reading has become one of the most vital fields of research in the humanities; yet it consists for the most part of case studies, which do not fit into a general pattern. Instead of sharing a common view of long-term trends, historians of reading tend to treat their subject as a moving target driven by the interplay of binary opposites: reading by turning the leaves of a codex as opposed to reading by unrolling a volumen, reading printed texts in contrast to reading manuscripts, silent reading as distinct from reading aloud, reading alone rather than reading in groups, reading extensively by racing through different kinds of material vs. reading intensively by perusing a few books many times. Now that the research has shifted to commonplace books, we may add segmental vs. sequential reading to the list.

More important, we may pay closer attention to reading as an element in what used to be called the history of mentalities — that is, world views and ways of thinking. All the keepers of commonplace books, from Drake to Madan, read their way through life, picking up fragments of experience and fitting them into patterns. The underlying affinities that held those patterns together represented an attempt to get a grip on life, to make sense of it, not by elaborating theories but by imposing form on matter. Commonplacing was like quilting: it produced pictures, some more beautiful than others, but each of them interesting in its own way. They reveal patterns of culture: the segments that went into it, the stitching that connected them, the tears that pulled them apart, and the common cloth of which they were composed.

CHAPTER 11

What Is the
History of Books?

This essay is an attempt, written thirty years ago, to describe the history of books as a new field of study and to suggest how its diverse aspects could be brought together in work on a common set of problems. Because it has touched off a considerable debate and has been widely assigned in courses, I was asked to reassess it in a sequel, "'What Is the History of Books?' Revisited," which appeared in Modern Intellectual History *(2007), vol. 4, pp. 495–508. The sequel puts the original essay in context and describes subsequent work, but I am reprinting only the earlier essay here.* *

"*HISTOIRE DU LIVRE*" in France, "*Geschichte des Buchwesens*" in Germany, "history of books" or "of the

---

*In order to avoid weighing it down with scholarly apparatus, I have eliminated all footnotes. They can be consulted along with the original text of the article, "What Is the History of Books?" in *Daedalus* (Summer 1982), pp. 65–83.

book" in English-speaking countries—its name varies from place to place, but everywhere it is being recognized as an important new discipline. It might even be called the social and cultural history of communication by print, if that were not such a mouthful, because its purpose is to understand how ideas were transmitted through print and how exposure to the printed word affected the thought and behavior of mankind during the last five hundred years. Some book historians pursue their subject deep into the period before the invention of movable type. Some students of printing concentrate on newspapers, broadsides, and other forms besides the book. The field can be extended and expanded in many ways; but for the most part, it concerns books since the time of Gutenberg, an area of research that has developed so rapidly during the last few years that it seems likely to win a place alongside fields like the history of science and the history of art in the canon of scholarly disciplines.

Whatever the history of books may become in the future, its past shows how a field of knowledge can take on a distinct scholarly identity. It arose from the convergence of several disciplines on a common set of problems, all of them having to do with the process of communication. Initially, the problems took the form of concrete questions in unrelated branches of scholarship: What were Shakespeare's original texts? What caused the French Revolution? What is the connection between culture and social stratification? In pursuing those questions, scholars found themselves crossing paths in a no-man's-land located at the intersection of a half-dozen fields of study. They decided to constitute a field of their own and to invite in historians, literary scholars, sociologists, librarians, and anyone else who wanted to understand the book as a force in history. The history of books began to acquire its own journals, research centers, conferences, and lecture circuits. It accumulated tribal elders as well as Young Turks. And although it has not yet developed passwords or secret handshakes or its own population of PhD's, its adherents can recognize one another by the glint in their eyes. They belong to a common cause, one of the few sectors in the human sciences where there is a mood of expansion and a flurry of fresh ideas.

To be sure, the history of the history of books did not begin yesterday. It stretches back to the scholarship of the Renaissance, if not beyond; and it began in earnest during the nineteenth century when the study of books as material objects led to the rise of analytical bibliography in England. But the current work represents a departure from the established strains of scholarship, which may be traced to their nineteenth-century origins through back issues of *The Library* and *Börsenblatt für den Deutschen Buchhandel* or theses in the Ecole des Chartes. The new strain developed during the 1960s in France, where it took root in institutions like the Ecole Pratique des Hautes Etudes and spread through publications like *L'Apparition du livre* (1958), by Lucien Febvre and Henri-Jean Martin, and *Livre et société dans la France du XVIII siècle* (two volumes 1965 and 1970) by a group connected with the VIème section of the Ecole Pratique des Hautes Etudes.

The new book historians brought the subject within the range of themes studied by the "*Annales* school" of socioeconomic history. Instead of dwelling on fine points of bibliography, they tried to uncover the general pattern of book production and consumption over long stretches of time. They compiled statistics from requests for *privilèges* (a kind of copyright), analyzed the contents of private libraries, and traced ideological currents through neglected genres like the *bibliothèque bleue* (primitive paperbacks). Rare books and fine editions had no interest for them; they concentrated instead on the most ordinary sort of books because they wanted to discover the literary experience of ordinary readers. They put familiar phenomena like the Counter Reformation and the Enlightenment in an unfamiliar light by showing how much traditional culture outweighed the avant-garde in the literary fare of the entire society. Although they did not come up with a firm set of conclusions, they demonstrated the importance of asking new questions, using new methods, and tapping new sources.

Their examples spread throughout Europe and the United States, reinforcing indigenous traditions, such as reception studies in Germany and printing history in Britain. Drawn together by their commitment to a common enterprise, and animated by enthusiasm for new ideas, book historians began to meet, first in cafés, then in conferences. They created new journals—*Publishing History, Bibliography Newsletter, Nouvelles du livre ancien, Revue française d'histoire du livre* (new series), *Buchhandelsgeschichte*, and *Wolfenbütteler Notizen zur Buchgeschichte*. They founded new centers—the Institut d'Etude du Livre in Paris, the Arbeitskreis für Geschichte des Buchwesens in Wolfenbüttel, the Center for the Book in the Library of Congress. Special colloquia—in Geneva, Paris, Boston, Worcester, Wolfenbüttel, and Athens, to name only a few that took place in the late 1970s—disseminated their research on an international scale. In the brief span of two decades, the history of books had become a rich and varied field of study.

So rich did it prove, in fact, that it now looks less like a field than a tropical rain forest. The explorer can hardly make his way across it. At every step he becomes entangled in a luxuriant undergrowth of journal articles and disoriented by the crisscrossing of disciplines—analytical bibliography pointing in this direction, the sociology of knowledge in that, while history, English, and comparative literature stake out overlapping territories. He is beset by claims to newness—*"la nouvelle bibliographie matérielle,"* "the new literary history"—and bewildered by competing methodologies, which would have him collating editions, compiling statistics, decoding copyright law, wading through reams of manuscript, heaving at the bar of a reconstructed common press, and psychoanalyzing the mental processes of readers. The history of books has become so crowded with ancillary disciplines that one can no longer see its general contours. How can the book historian neglect the history of libraries, of publishing, of paper, type, and reading? But how can he master their technologies, especially when they appear in imposing foreign formulations, like *Geschichte der Appellstruktur* and *Bibliométrie bibliologique?* It is enough to make one want to retire to a rare-book room and count watermarks.

To get some distance from interdisciplinarity run riot, and to see the subject as a whole, it might be useful to propose a general model for analyzing the way books come into being and spread through society. To be sure, conditions have varied so much from place to place and from time to time since the invention of movable type that it would be vain to expect the biography of every book to conform to the same pattern. But printed books generally pass through roughly the same life cycle. It could be described as a communications circuit that runs from the author to the publisher (if the bookseller does not assume that role), the printer, the shipper, the bookseller, and the reader. The reader completes the circuit because he influences the author both before and after the act of composition. Authors are readers themselves. By reading and associating with other readers and writers, they form notions of genre and style and a general sense of the literary enterprise, which affects their texts, whether they are composing Shakespearean sonnets or directions for assembling radio kits. A writer may respond in his writing to criticisms of his previous work or anticipate reactions that his text will elicit. He addresses implicit readers and hears from explicit reviewers. So the circuit runs full cycle. It transmits messages, transforming them en route, as they pass from thought to writing to printed characters and back to thought again. Book history concerns each phase of this process and the process as a whole, in all its variations over space and time and in all its relations with other systems, economic, social, political, and cultural, in the surrounding environment.

That is a large undertaking. To keep their task within manageable proportions, book historians generally cut into one segment of the communications circuit and analyze it according to the procedures of a single discipline—printing, for example, which they study by means of analytical bibliography. But the parts do not take on their full significance unless they are related to the whole, and some holistic view of the book as a means of communication seems necessary if book history is to avoid being fragmented into esoteric specializations cut off from each other by arcane techniques and mutual misunderstanding. The model shown in the figure on page 182 provides a way of envisaging the entire communication process. With minor adjustments, it should apply to all periods in the history of the printed book (manuscript books and book illustrations will need to be considered elsewhere), but I would like to discuss the connection with the period I know best, the eighteenth century, and to take it up phase by phase, showing how each phase is related to (1) other activities that a given person has underway at a given point in the circuit, (2) other persons at the same point in other circuits, (3) other persons at other points in the same circuit, and (4) other elements in society. The first three considerations bear directly on the transmission of a text, while the last concerns outside influences, which could vary endlessly. For the sake of simplicity, I have reduced the latter to the three general categories in the center of the diagram.

Models have a way of freezing human beings out of history. To put some flesh and blood on this one, and to show how it can make sense of an actual case, I will apply it to the publishing history of Voltaire's *Questions sur l'Encyclopédie*, an important work of the Enlightenment, and one that touched the lives of a great many eighteenth-century bookmen. One could study the circuit of its transmission at any point—at the stage of its composition, for example, when Voltaire shaped its text and orchestrated its diffusion in order to promote his campaign against religious intolerance, as his biographers have shown; or at its printing, a stage in which bibliographical analysis helps to establish the multiplication of editions; or at the point of its assimilation in libraries, where, according to statistical studies by literary historians, Voltaire's works occupied an impressive share of shelf space. But I would like to concentrate on the least familiar link in the diffusion process, the role of the bookseller, taking Isaac-Pierre Rigaud of Montpellier as an example, and working through the four considerations mentioned above.

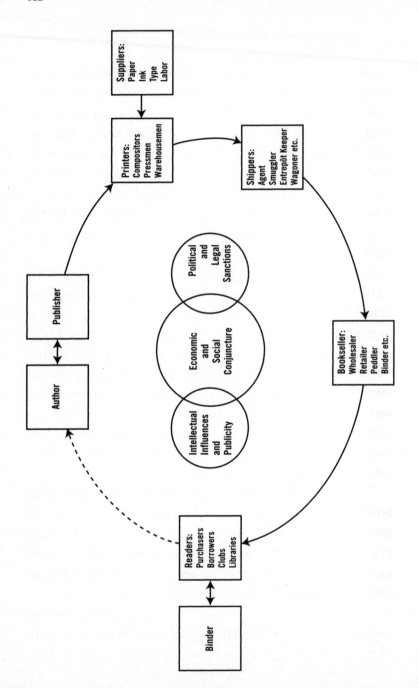

I

On August 16, 1770, Rigaud ordered thirty copies of the nine-volume octavo edition of the *Questions*, which the Société typographique dc Neuchâtel (STN) had recently begun to print in the Prussian principality of Neuchâtel on the Swiss side of the French-Swiss border. Rigaud generally preferred to read at least a few pages of a new book before stocking it, but he consider the *Questions* such a good bet that he risked making a fairly large order for it, sight unseen. He did not have any personal sympathy for Voltaire. On the contrary, he deplored the philosophe's tendency to tinker with his books, adding and amending passages while cooperating with pirated editions behind the backs of the original publishers. Such practices produced complaints from customers, who objected to receiving inferior (or insufficiently audacious) texts. "It is astonishing that at the end of his career M. de Voltaire cannot refrain from duping booksellers," Rigaud complained to the STN. "It would not matter if all these little ruses, frauds, and deceits were blamed on the author. But unfortunately the printers and still more the retail booksellers are usually held responsible." Voltaire made life hard for booksellers, but he sold well.

There was nothing Voltairean about most of the other books in Rigaud's shop. His sales catalogues show that he specialized somewhat in medical books, which were always in demand in Montpellier, thanks to the university's famous faculty of medicine. Rigaud also kept a discreet line of Protestant works, because Montpellier lay in Huguenot territory. And when the authorities looked the other way, he brought in a few shipments of forbidden books. But he generally supplied his customers with books of all kinds, which he drew from an inventory worth at least forty-five thousand livres, the largest in Montpellier and probably in all Languedoc, according to a report from the intendant's *subdélégué*.

Rigaud's way of ordering from the STN illustrates the character of his business. Unlike other large provincial dealers, who speculated on a hundred or more copies of a book when they smelled a best seller, he rarely ordered more than a half dozen copies of a single work. He read widely, consulted his customers, took soundings by means of his commercial correspondence, and studied the catalogues that the STN and his other suppliers sent to him (by 1785 the STN's catalogue included seven hundred and fifty titles). Then he chose about ten titles and ordered just enough copies of them to make up a crate of fifty pounds, the minimum weight for shipment at the cheaper rate charged by the wagoners. If the books sold well, he reordered them; but he usually kept his orders rather small, and made four or five of them a year. In this way, he conserved capital, minimized risks, and built up such a large and varied stock that his shop became a clearinghouse for literary demand of every kind in the region.

The pattern of Rigaud's orders, which stands out clearly from the STN's account books, shows that he offered his customers a little of everything—travel books, histories, novels, religious works, and the occasional scientific or philosophical treatise. Instead of following his own preferences, he seemed to transmit demand fairly accurately and to live according to the accepted wisdom of the book trade, which one of the STN's other customers summarized as follows: "The best book for a bookseller is a book that sells." Given his cautious style of business, Rigaud's decision to place an advance order for thirty nine-volume sets of the *Questions sur l'Encyclopédie* seems especially significant. He would not have put so much money on a single work if he had not felt certain of the demand—and his later orders show that he had calculated correctly. On June 19, 1772, soon after receiving the last shipment of the last volume, Rigaud ordered another dozen sets; and he ordered two more two years later, although by then the STN had exhausted its stock. It had printed a huge edition, twenty-five hundred copies, approximately twice its usual press run, and the booksellers had fallen all over themselves in the rush to purchase it. So Rigaud's purchase was no aberration. It expressed a current of Voltaireanism that had spread far and wide among the reading public of the Old Regime.

II

How does the purchase of the *Questions* look when examined from the perspective of Rigaud's relations with the other booksellers of Montpellier? A book-trade almanac listed nine of them in 1777.

Printer-Booksellers:
   Aug. Franç. Rochard
   Jean Martel
Booksellers:
   Isaac-Pierre Rigaud
   J. B. Faure
   Albert Pons
   Tournel
   Bascon
   Cézary
   Fontanel

But according to a report from a traveling salesman of the STN, there were only seven. Rigaud and Pons had merged and completely dominated the local trade; Cézary and Faure scraped along in the middle ranks; and the rest teetered on the brink of bankruptcy in precarious boutiques. The occasional binder and under-the-cloak peddler also provided a few books, most of them illegal, to the more adventuresome readers of the city. For example, the demoiselle Bringand, known as "the students' mother," stocked some forbidden fruit "under the bed on the room to the right on the second floor," according to the report of a raid that was engineered by the established booksellers. The trade in most provincial cities fell into the same pattern, which can be envisaged as a series of concentric circles: at the center, one or two firms tried to monopolize the market; around the margin, a few small dealers survived by specializing in chapbooks and old volumes, by setting up reading clubs *(cabinets littéraires)* and binderies, or by peddling their wares in the back country; and beyond the fringe of legality, adventurers moved in and out of the market, selling forbidden literature.

When he ordered his shipment of the *Questions*, Rigaud was consolidating his position at the center of the local trade. His merger with Pons in 1770 provided him with enough capital and assets to ride out the mishaps—delayed shipments, defaulting debtors, liquidity crises—that often upset smaller businesses. Also, he played rough. When Cézary, one of the middling dealers, failed to meet some of his payments in 1781, Rigaud drove him out of business by organizing a cabal of his creditors. They refused to let him reschedule the payments, had him thrown in prison for debt, and forced him to sell off his stock at an auction, where they kept down the prices and gobbled up the books. By dispensing patronage, Rigaud controlled most of Montpellier's binderies; and by exerting pressure on the binders, he produced delays and snags in the affairs of the other booksellers. In 1789 only one of them remained, Abraham Fontanel, and he stayed solvent only by maintaining a *cabinet littéraire*, "which provokes terrible fits of jealousy by the sieur Rigaud, who wants to be the only one left and who shows his hatred of me every day," as Fontanel confided to the STN.

Rigaud did not eliminate his competitors simply by outdoing them in the dog-eat-dog style of commercial capitalism of early modern France. His letters, theirs, and the correspondence of many other booksellers show that the book trade contracted during the late 1770s and 1780s. In hard times, the big booksellers squeezed out the small, and the tough outlasted the tender. Rigaud had been a tough customer from the very beginning of his relations with the STN. He had ordered his copies of the *Questions* from Neuchâtel, where the STN was printing a pirated edition, rather than from Geneva, where Voltaire's regular printer, Gabriel Cramer, was producing the original, because he had extracted better terms. He also demanded better service, especially when the other booksellers in Montpellier, who had dealt with Cramer, received their copies first. The delay produced a volley of letters from Rigaud to the STN. Why couldn't the STN work faster? Didn't it know that it was making him lose customers to his competitors? He would have to order from Cramer in the future if it could not provide quicker shipments at a lower price. When volumes one through three finally arrived from Neuchâtel, volumes four through six from Geneva were already on sale in the other shops. Rigaud compared the texts, word for word, and found that the STN's edition contained none of the additional material that it had claimed to receive on the sly from Voltaire. So how could he push the theme of "additions and corrections" in his sales talk? The recriminations flew thick and fast in the mail between Montpellier and Neuchâtel, and they showed that Rigaud meant to exploit every inch of every advantage that he could gain on his competitors. More important, they also revealed that the *Questions* were being sold all over Montpellier, even though in principle they could not circulate legally in France. Far from being confined to the under-the-cloak trade of marginal characters like "the students' mother," Voltaire's work turned out to be a prize item in the scramble for profits at the very heart of the established book trade. When dealers like Rigaud scratched and clawed for their shipments of it, Voltaire could be sure that he was succeeding in his attempt to propel his ideas through the main lines of France's communications system.

III

The role of Voltaire and Cramer in the diffusion process raises the problem of how Rigaud's operation fit into the other stages in the life cycle of the *Questions*. Rigaud knew that he was not getting a first edition; the STN had sent a circular letter to him and its other main customers explaining that it would reproduce Cramer's text, but with corrections and additions provided by the author himself, so that its version would be superior to the original. One of the STN's directors had visited Voltaire at Ferney in April 1770 and had returned with a promise that Voltaire would touch up the printed sheets he was to receive from Cramer and then would forward them to Neuchâtel for a pirated edition. Voltaire often played such tricks. They provided a way to improve the quality and increase the quantity of his books, and therefore served his main purpose—which was not to make money, for he did not sell his prose to the printers, but to spread Enlightenment. The profit motive kept the rest of the system going, however. So when Cramer got wind of the STN's attempt to raid his market, he protested to Voltaire, Voltaire retracted his promise to the STN, and the STN had to settle for a delayed version of the text, which it received from Ferney, but with only minimal additions and corrections. In fact, this setback did not hurt its sales, because the market had plenty of room to absorb editions, not only the STN's but also one that Marc Michel Rey produced in Amsterdam, and probably others as well. The booksellers had their choice of suppliers, and they chose according to whatever marginal advantage they could obtain on matters of price, quality, speed, and reliability in delivery. Rigaud dealt regularly with publishers in Paris, Lyon, Rouen, Avignon, and Geneva. He played them off against each other and sometimes ordered the same book from two or three of them so as to be certain of getting it before his competitors did. By working several circuits at the same time, he increased his room for maneuver. But in the case of the *Questions*, he was outmaneuvered and had to receive his goods from the circuitous Voltaire-Cramer-Voltaire-STN route.

That route merely took the copy from the author to the printer. For the printed sheets to reach Rigaud in Montpellier from the STN's shop in Neuchâtel, they had to wind their way through one of the most complex stages in the book's circuit. They could follow two main routes. One led from Neuchâtel to Geneva, Turin, Nice (which was not yet French), and Marseilles. It had the advantage of skirting

French territory—and therefore the danger of confiscation—but it involved huge detours and expenses. The books had to be lugged over the Alps and pass through a whole army of middlemen—shipping agents, bargemen, wagoners, entrepôt keepers, ship captains, and dockers—before they arrived in Rigaud's storeroom. The best Swiss shippers claimed they could get a craft to Nice in a month for thirteen livres, eight sous per hundredweight; but their estimates proved to be far too low. The direct route from Neuchâtel to Lyon and down the Rhône was fast, cheap, and easy—but dangerous. The crates had to be sealed at their point of entry into France and inspected by the booksellers' guild and the royal book inspector in Lyon, then reshipped and inspected once more in Montpellier.

Always cautious, Rigaud asked the STN to ship the first volumes of the *Questions* by the roundabout route, because he knew he could rely on his agent in Marseilles, Joseph Coulomb, to get the books into France without mishap. They left on December 9, 1771, but did not arrive until after March, when the first three volumes of Cramer's edition were already being sold by Rigaud's competitors. The second and third volumes arrived in July, but loaded down with shipping charges and damaged by rough handling. "It seems that we are five or six thousand leagues apart," Rigaud complained, adding that he regretted he had not given his business to Cramer, whose shipments had already reached volume six. By this time, the STN was worried enough about losing customers throughout southern France to set up a smuggling operation in Lyon. Their man, a marginal bookdealer named Joseph-Louis Berthoud, got volumes four and five past the guild inspectors, but then his business collapsed in bankruptcy; and to make matters worse, the French government imposed a tax of sixty livres per hundredweight on all book imports. The STN fell back on the Alpine route, offering to get its shipments as far as Nice for fifteen livres per hundredweight if Rigaud would pay the rest of the expenses, including the import duty. But Rigaud considered the duty such a heavy blow to the international trade that he suspended all his orders with foreign suppliers. The new tariff policy had made it prohibitively expensive to disguise illegal books as legal ones and to pass them through normal commercial channels.

In December, the STN's agent in Nice, Jacques Deandreis, somehow got a shipment of volume six of the *Questions* to Rigaud through the port of Sète, which was supposed to be closed to book imports. Then the French government, realizing that it had nearly destroyed the foreign book trade, lowered the tariff to twenty-six livres per hundredweight. Rigaud proposed sharing the cost with his suppliers: he would pay one third if they would pay two thirds. This proposal suited the STN, but in the spring of 1772 Rigaud decided that the Nice route was too expensive to be used under any conditions. Having heard enough complaints from its other customers to reach the same conclusion, the STN dispatched one of its directors to Lyon, and he persuaded a more dependable Lyonnais dealer, J.-M. Barret, to clear its shipments through the local guild and forward them to its provincial clients. Thanks to this arrangement, the last three volumes of Rigaud's *Questions* arrived safely in the summer.

It had required continuous effort and considerable expense to get the entire order to Montpellier, and Rigaud and the STN did not stop realigning their supply routes once they had completed this transaction. Because economic and political pressures kept shifting, they had constantly to readjust their arrangements within the complex world of middlemen, who linked printing houses with bookshops and often determined, in the last analysis, what literature reached French readers.

How the readers assimilated their books cannot be determined. Bibliographical analysis of all the copies that can be located would show what varieties of the text were available. A study of notarial archives in Montpellier might indicate how many copies turned up in inheritances, and statistics drawn from auction catalogues might make it possible to estimate the number in substantial private libraries. But given the present state of documentation, one cannot know who Voltaire's readers were or how they responded to his text. Reading remains the most difficult stage to study in the circuit that books follow.

IV

All stages were affected by the social, economic, political, and intellectual conditions of the time; but for Rigaud, these general influences made themselves felt within a local context. He sold books in a city of thirty-one thousand inhabitants. Despite an important textile industry, Montpellier was essentially an old-fashioned administrative and religious center, richly endowed with cultural institutions, including a university, an academy of sciences, twelve Masonic lodges, and sixteen monastic communities. And because it was a seat of the provincial estates of Languedoc and an intendancy, and had as well an array of courts, the city had a large population of lawyers and royal officials. If they resembled their counterparts in other provincial centers, they probably provided Rigaud with a good many of his cus-

tomers and probably had a taste for Enlightenment literature. He did not discuss their social background in his correspondence, but he noted that they clamored for the works
of Voltaire, Rousseau, and Raynal. They subscribed heavily
to the *Encyclopédie*, and even asked for atheistic treatises
like *Système de la nature* and *Philosophie de la nature*.
Montpellier was no intellectual backwater, and it was good
book territory. "The book trade is quite extensive in this
town," an observer remarked in 1768. "The booksellers
have kept their shops well stocked ever since the inhabitants
developed a taste for having libraries."

These favorable conditions prevailed when Rigaud ordered his *Questions*. But hard times set in during the early
1770s; and in the 1780s Rigaud, like most booksellers, complained of a severe decline in his trade. The whole French
economy contracted during those years, according to the
standard account of C. E. Labrousse. Certainly, the state's finances went into a tailspin: hence the disastrous book tariff
of 1771, which belonged to the unsuccessful attempt of the
controller general of finance, abbé Joseph Marie Terray, to
reduce the deficit accumulated during the Seven Years' War.
The government also tried to stamp out pirated and forbidden books, first by more severe police work in 1771–74, then
by a general reform of the book trade in 1777. These measures eventually ruined Rigaud's commerce with the STN and
with the other publishing houses that had grown up around
France's borders during the prosperous mid-century years.
Foreign publishers produced both original editions of books
that could not pass the censorship in Paris and pirated editions
of books put out by the Parisian publishers. Because the
Parisians had acquired a virtual monopoly over the legal publishing industry, their rivals in the provinces formed alliances

with the foreign houses and looked the other way when shipments from abroad arrived for inspection in the provincial guild halls *(chambres syndicales)*. Under Louis XIV, the government had used the Parisian guild as an instrument to suppress the illegal trade: but under Louis XV it became increasingly lax, until a new era of severity began with the fall of the duc de Choiseul's ministry (December 1770). Thus Rigaud's relations with the STN fit perfectly into an economic and political pattern that had prevailed in the book trade since the early eighteenth century and that began to fall apart just as the first crates of the *Questions* were making their way between Neuchâtel and Montpellier.

Other patterns might show up in other research, for the model need not be applied in this manner, nor need it be applied at all. I am not arguing that book history should be written according to a standard formula but trying to show how its disparate segments can be brought together within a single conceptual scheme. Different book historians might prefer different schemata. They might concentrate on the book trade of all Languedoc, as Madeleine Ventre has done; or on the general bibliography of Voltaire, as Giles Barber, Jeroom Vercruysse, and others are doing; or on the overall pattern of book production in eighteenth-century France, in the manner of François Furet and Robert Estivals. But however they define their subject, they will not draw out its full significance unless they relate it to all the elements that worked together as a circuit for transmitting texts. To make the point clearer, I will go over the model circuit once more, noting questions that have been investigated successfully or that seem ripe for further research.

I *AUTHORS*

Despite the proliferation of biographies of great writers, the basic conditions of authorship remain obscure for most periods of history. At what point did writers free themselves from the patronage of wealthy noblemen and the state in order to live by their pens? What was the nature of a literary career, and how was it pursued? How did writers deal with publishers, printers, booksellers, reviewers, and one another? Until those questions are answered, we will not have a full understanding of the transmission of texts. Voltaire was able to manipulate secret alliances with pirate publishers because he did not depend on writing for a living. A century later, Zola proclaimed that a writer's independence came from selling his prose to the highest bidder. How did this transformation take place? The work of John Lough begins to provide an answer, but more systematic research on the evolution of the republic of letters in France could be done from police records, literary almanacs, and bibliographies (*La France littéraire* gives the names and publications of 1,187 writers in 1757 and 3,089 in 1784). The situation in Germany is more obscure, owing to the fragmentation of the German states before 1871. But German scholars are beginning to tap sources like *Das gelehrte Teutschland*, which lists four thousand writers in 1779, and to trace the links between authors, publishers, and readers in regional and monographic studies. Marino Berengo has shown how much can be discovered about author-publisher relations in Italy. And the work of A. S. Collins still provides an excellent account of authorship in England, although it needs to be brought up-to-date and extended beyond the eighteenth century.

II *PUBLISHERS*

The key role of publishers is now becoming clearer, thanks to articles appearing in the *Journal of Publishing History* and monographs like Martin Lowry's *The World of Aldus Manutius*, Robert Patten's *Charles Dickens and His Publishers*, and Gary Stark's *Entrepreneurs of Ideology: Neoconservative Publishers in Germany, 1890–1933*. But the evolution of the publisher as a distinct figure in contrast to the master bookseller and the printer still needs systematic study. Historians have barely begun to tap the papers of publishers, although they are the richest of all sources for the history of books. The archives of the Cotta Verlag in Marbach, for example, contain at least one hundred fifty thousand documents, yet they have only been skimmed for references to Goethe, Schiller, and other famous writers. Further investigation almost certainly would turn up a great deal of information about the book as a force in nineteenth-century Germany. How did publishers draw up contracts with authors, build alliances with booksellers, negotiate with political authorities, and handle finances, supplies, shipments, and publicity? The answers to those questions would carry the history of books deep into the territory of social, economic, and political history, to their mutual benefit.

The Project for Historical Biobibliography at Newcastle upon Tyne and the Institut de Littérature et de Techniques Artistiques de Masse at Bordeaux illustrate the directions that such interdisciplinary work has already taken. The Bordeaux group has tried to trace books through different distribution systems in order to uncover the literary experience of different groups in contemporary France. The researchers in Newcastle have studied the diffusion process through quantitative analysis of subscription lists, which were widely used in the sales campaigns of British publishers from the early seventcenth to the early nineteenth centuries. Similar work could be done on publishers' catalogues and prospectuses, which have been collected in research centers like the Newberry Library. The whole subject of book advertising needs investigation. One could learn a great deal about attitudes toward books and the context of their use by studying the way they were presented—the strategy of the appeal, the values invoked by the phrasing—in all kinds of publicity, from journal notices to wall posters. American historians have used newspaper advertisements to map the spread of the printed word into the back reaches of colonial society. By consulting the papers of publishers, they could make deeper inroads in the nineteenth and twentieth centuries. Unfortunately, however, publishers usually treat their archives as garbage. Although they save the occasional letter from a famous author, they throw away account books and commercial correspondence, which usually are the most important sources of information for the book historian. The Center for the Book in the Library of Congress is now compiling a guide to publishers' archives. If they can be preserved and studied, they might provide a different perspective on the whole course of American history.

III *PRINTERS*

The printing shop is far better known than the other stages in the production and diffusion of books because it has been a favorite subject of study in the field of analytical bibliography, whose purpose, as defined by R. B. McKerrow and Philip Gaskell, is "to elucidate the transmission of texts by explaining the processes of book production." Bibliographers have made important contributions to textual criticism, especially in Shakespearean scholarship, by building inferences backward from the structure of a book to the process of its printing and hence to an original text, such as the missing Shakespeare manuscripts. That line of reasoning has been undercut recently by D. F. McKenzie. But even if they can never reconstruct an ur-Shakespeare, bibliographers can demonstrate the existence of different editions of a text and of different states of an edition, a necessary skill in diffusion studies. Their techniques also make it possible to decipher the records of printers and so have opened up a new, archival phase in the history of printing. Thanks to the work of McKenzie, Leon Voet, Raymond de Roover, and Jacques Rychner, we now have a clear picture of how printing shops operated throughout the hand-press period (roughly 1500–1800). More work needs to be done on later periods, and new questions could be asked: How did printers calculate costs and organize production, especially after the spread of job printing and journalism? How did book budgets change after the introduction of machine-made paper in the first decade of the nineteenth century and Linotype in the 1880s? How did the technological changes affect the management of labor? And what part did journeymen printers, an unusually articulate and militant sector of the working class, play in labor history? Analytical bibliography may seem arcane to the outsider, but it could make a great contribution to social as well as literary history, especially if it were seasoned with a reading of printers' manuals and autobiographies, beginning with those of Thomas Platter, Thomas Gent, N. E. Restif de la Bretonne, Benjamin Franklin, and Charles Manby Smith.

IV *SHIPPERS*

Little is known about the way books reached bookstores from printing shops. The wagon, the canal barge, the merchant vessel, the post office, and the railroad may have influenced the history of literature more than one would suspect. Although transport facilities probably had little effect on the trade in great publishing centers like London and Paris, they sometimes determined the ebb and flow of business in remote areas. Before the nineteenth century, books were usually sent in sheets, so that the customer could have them bound according to his taste and his ability to pay. They traveled in large bales wrapped in heavy paper and were easily damaged by rain and the friction of ropes. Compared with commodities like textiles, their intrinsic value was slight, yet their shipping costs were high, owing to the size and weight of the sheets. So shipping often took up a large proportion of a book's total cost and a large place in the marketing strategy of publishers. In many parts of Europe, printers could not count on getting shipments to booksellers in August and September because wagoners abandoned their routes to work the harvest. The Baltic trade frequently ground to a halt after October, because ice closed the ports. Routes opened and shut everywhere in response to the pressures of war, politics, and even insurance rates. Unorthodox literature has traveled underground in huge quantities from the sixteenth century to the present, so its influence has varied according to the effectiveness of the smuggling industry. And other genres, like chapbooks and penny dreadfuls, circulated through special distribution systems, which need much more study, although book historians are now beginning to clear some of the ground.

V *BOOKSELLERS*

Thanks to some classic studies—H. W. Bennett on early modern England, L. C. Wroth on colonial America, H.-J. Martin on seventeenth-century France, and Johann Goldfriedrich on Germany—it is possible to piece together a general picture of the evolution of the book trade. But more work needs to be done on the bookseller as a cultural agent, the middleman who mediated between supply and demand at their key point of contact. We still do not know enough about the social and intellectual world of men like Rigaud, about their values and tastes and the way they fit into their communities. They also operated within commercial networks, which expanded and collapsed like alliances in the diplomatic world. What laws governed the rise and fall of trade empires in publishing? A comparison of national histories could reveal some general tendencies, such as the centripetal force of great centers like London, Paris, Frankfurt, and Leipzig, which drew provincial houses into their orbits, and the countervailing trend toward alignments between provincial dealers and suppliers in independent enclaves like Liège, Bouillon, Neuchâtel, Geneva, and Avignon. But comparisons are difficult because the trade operated through different institutions in different countries, which generated different kinds of archives. The records of the London Stationers' Company, the Communauté des Libraires et Imprimeurs de Paris, and the Leipzig and Frankfurt book fairs have had a great deal to do with the different courses that book history has taken in England, France, and Germany.

Nevertheless, books were sold as commodities everywhere. A more unabashedly economic study of them would provide a new perspective to the history of literature. James Barnes,

John Tebbel, and Frédéric Barbier have demonstrated the importance of the economic element in the book trades of nineteenth-century England, America, and France. But more work could be done—on credit mechanisms, for example, and the techniques of negotiating bills of exchange, of defense against suspensions of payment, and of exchanging printed sheets in lieu of payment in specie. The book trade, like other businesses during the Renaissance, and early modern periods, was largely a confidence game, but we still do not know how it was played.

VI *READERS*

Despite a considerable literature on its psychology, phenomenology, textology, and sociology, reading remains mysterious. How do readers make sense of the signs on the printed page? What are the social effects of that experience? And how has it varied? Literary scholars like Wayne Booth, Stanley Fish, Wolfgang Iser, Walter Ong, and Jonathan Culler have made reading a central concern of textual criticism because they understand literature as an activity, the construal of meaning within a system of communication, rather than a canon of texts. The book historian could make use of their notions of fictitious audiences, implicit readers, and interpretive communities. But he may find their observations somewhat time-bound. Although the critics know their way around literary history (they are especially strong on seventeenth-century England), they seem to assume that texts have always worked on the sensibilities of readers in the same way. But a seventeenth-century London burgher inhabited a different mental universe from that of a twentieth-century

American professor. Reading itself has changed over time. It was often done aloud and in groups, or in secret and with an intensity we may not be able to imagine today. Carlo Ginsburg has shown how much meaning a sixteenth-century miller could infuse into a text, and Margaret Spufford has demonstrated that still humbler workmen fought their way to mastery over the printed word in the era of *Areopagitica*. Everywhere in early modern Europe, from the ranks of Montaigne to those of Menocchio, readers wrung significance from books; they did not merely decipher them. Reading was a passion long before the *"Lesewut"* and the *"Wertherfieber"* of the romantic era; and there is *Sturm und Drang* in it yet, despite the vogue for speed-reading and the mechanistic view of literature as the encoding and decoding of messages.

But texts shape the response of readers, however active they may be. As Walter Ong has observed, the opening pages of *The Canterbury Tales* and *A Farewell to Arms* create a frame and cast the reader in a role, which he cannot avoid no matter what he thinks of pilgrimages and civil wars. In fact, typography as well as style and syntax determine the ways in which texts convey meanings. McKenzie has shown that the bawdy, unruly Congreve of the early quarto editions settled down into the decorous neoclassicist of the *Works* of 1710 as a consequence of book design rather than bowdlerization. The history of reading will have to take account of the ways that texts constrain readers as well as the ways that readers take liberties with texts. The tension between those tendencies has existed wherever men confronted books, and it has produced some extraordinary results, as in Luther's reading of Paul's Epistles, Rousseau's reading of *Le Misanthrope*, and Kierkegaard's reading of the sacrifice of Isaac.

If it is possible to recapture the great rereadings of the past, the inner experience of ordinary readers may always elude us. But we should at least be able to reconstruct a good deal of the social context of reading. The debate about silent reading during the Middle Ages has produced some impressive evidence about reading habits; and studies of reading societies in Germany, where they proliferated to an extraordinary degree in the eighteenth and nineteenth centuries, have shown the importance of reading in the development of a distinct bourgeois cultural style. German scholars have also done a great deal in the history of libraries and in reception studies of all kinds. Following a notion of Rolf Engelsing, they often maintain that reading habits became transformed at the end of the eighteenth century. Before this *"Leserevolution,"* readers tended to work laboriously through a small number of texts, especially the Bible, over and over again. Afterwards, they raced through all kinds of material, seeking amusement rather than edification. The shift from intensive to extensive reading coincided with a desacralization of the printed word. The world began to be cluttered with reading matter, and texts began to be treated as commodities that could be discarded as casually as yesterday's newspaper. This interpretation has recently been disputed by Reinhart Siegert, Martin Welke, and other young scholars, who have discovered "intensive" reading in the reception of fugitive works like almanacs and newspapers, notably the *Noth-und Hülfsbüchlein* of Rudolph Zacharias Becker, an extraordinary best seller of the *Goethezeit*. But whether or not the concept of a reading revolution will hold up, it has helped to align research on reading with general questions of social and cultural history. The same can be said of research on literacy, which has made it possible for scholars to detect the vague outline of diverse reading publics two and three centuries ago and to trace books to readers at several levels of society. The lower the level, the more intense the study. Popular literature has been a favorite topic of research during the last decade, despite a growing tendency to question the notion that cheap booklets like the *bibliothèque bleue* represented an autonomous culture of the common people or that one can distinguish clearly between strains of "elite" and "popular" culture. It now seems inadequate to view cultural change as a linear, or trickle-down, movement of influences. Currents flowed up as well as down, merging and blending as they went. Characters like Gargantua, Cinderella, and Buscon moved back and forth through oral traditions, chapbooks, and sophisticated literature, changing in nationality as well as genre. One could even trace the metamorphoses of stock figures in almanacs. What does Poor Richard's reincarnation as *le Bonhomme Richard* reveal about literary culture in America and France? And what can be learned about German-French relations by following the Lame Messenger *(der hinkende Bote, le messager boiteux)* through the traffic of almanacs across the Rhine?

Questions about who reads what, in what conditions, at what time, and with what effect, link reading studies with sociology. The book historian could learn how to pursue such questions from the work of Douglas Waples, Bernard Berelson, Paul Lazarsfeld, and Pierre Bourdieu. He could draw on the reading research that flourished in the Graduate Library School of the University of Chicago from 1930 to 1950, and that still turns up in the occasional Gallup report. And as an example of the sociological strain in historical writing, he could consult the studies of reading (and nonreading) in the English working class during the last two centuries by Richard Altick, Robert Webb, and Richard Hoggart. All this work opens onto the larger problem of how exposure to the printed word affects the way men think. Did the invention of movable type transform man's mental universe? There may be no single satisfactory answer to that question because it bears on so many different aspects of life in early modern Europe, as Elizabeth Eisenstein has shown. But it should be possible to arrive at a firmer understanding of what books meant to people. Their use in the taking of oaths, the exchanging of gifts, the awarding of prizes, and the bestowing of legacies would provide clues to their significance within different societies. The iconography of books could indicate the weight of their authority, even for illiterate laborers who sat in church before pictures of the tablets of Moses. The place of books in folklore, and of folk motifs in books, shows that influences ran both ways when oral traditions came into contact with printed texts, and that books need to be studied in relation to other media. The lines of research could lead in many directions, but they all should issue ultimately in a larger understanding of how printing has shaped man's attempts to make sense of the human condition.

One can easily lose sight of the larger dimensions of the enterprise because book historians often stray into esoteric byways and unconnected specializations. Their work can be so fragmented, even within the limits of the literature on a single country, that it may seem hopeless to conceive of book history as a single subject, to be studied from a comparative perspective across the whole range of historical disciplines. But books themselves do not respect limits either linguistic or national. They have often been written by authors who belonged to an international republic of letters, composed by printers who did not work in their native tongue, sold by booksellers who operated across national boundaries, and read in one language by readers who spoke another. Books also refuse to be contained within the confines of a single discipline when treated as objects of study. Neither history nor literature nor economics nor sociology nor bibliography can do justice to all aspects of the life of a book. By its very nature, therefore, the history of books must be international in scale and interdisciplinary in method. But it need not lack conceptual coherence, because books belong to circuits of communication that operate in consistent patterns, however complex they may be. By unearthing those circuits, historians can show that books do not merely recount history; they make it.

BIBLIOGRAPHY

Baker, Nicholson. *Double Fold: Libraries and the Assault on Paper*. New York: Random House, 2001.

Bowers, Fredson. *Principles of Bibliographical Description*. Princeton, NJ: Princeton University Press, 1949.

Gallup-Diaz, Ignacio. *The Door of the Seas and Key to the Universe: Indian Politics and the Imperial Rivalry in the Darien, 1640–1750*. New York: Columbia University Press, 2001.

Gaskell, Philip. *A New Introduction to Bibliography*. Oxford, UK: Clarendon Press, 1972.

Gengenbach, Heidi. *Binding Memories: Women as Makers and Tellers of History in Magude, Mozambique*. West Sussex, NY: Columbia University Press, 2005.

Gere, J. A., and John Sparrow, eds. *Geoffrey Madan's Notebooks*. Oxford, UK, and New York: Oxford University Press, 1981, reprinted in 1985.

Hinman, Charlton. *The Printing and Proof-Reading of the First Folio of Shakespeare*. Oxford, UK: Clarendon Press, 1963.

Lockridge, Kenneth A. *On the Sources of Patriarchal Rage. The Commonplace Books of William Byrd and Thomas Jefferson and the Gendering of Power in the Eighteenth Century*. New York: New York University Press, 1992.

Lowry, Martin. *The World of Aldus Manutius: Business and Scholarship in Renaissance Venice*. London: Blackwell, 1979.

McKenzie, D. F. *Making Meaning. "Printers of the Mind" and Other Essays*, edited by Peter D. McDonald and Michael F. Suarez, S.J. Amherst and Boston: University of Massachusetts Press, 2002.

McKenzie, Donald F. *The Cambridge University Press, 1696–1712*. Cambridge, UK: Cambridge University Press, 1966.

McKerrow, R. B. *An Introduction to Bibliography for Literary Students.* Oxford, UK: Clarendon Press, 1928.

Norton, Mary Beth, and Pamela Gerardi, eds. *The American Historical Association's Guide to Historical Literature.* 2 vols. New York: Oxford University Press, 1995.

Orgel, Stephen, and A. R. Braunmuller, eds. *The Complete Pelican Shakespeare.* London and New York: Penguin, 2002.

Patten, Robert L., and Robert Patten. *Charles Dickens and His Publishers.* Santa Cruz: Dickens Project, University of California, 1991.

Sharpe, Kevin. *Reading Revolutions. The Politics of Reading in Early Modern England.* New Haven, CT: Yale University Press, 2000.

Stark, Gary D. *Entrepreneurs of Ideology: Neoconservative Publishers in Germany, 1890–1933.* University of North Carolina, 1981.

Thomson, John, ed. *Books & Bibliography: Essays in Commemoration of Don McKenzie.* Wellington, New Zealand: Victoria University Press, 2002.

Wells, Stanley, and Gary Taylor, eds. *The Complete Oxford Shakespeare.* Oxford, UK: Oxford University Press, 1987.

Wilson, Douglas L. *Jefferson's Literary Commonplace Book.* Princeton, NJ: Princeton University Press, 1989.

Wilson, F. P. *Shakespeare and the New Bibliography.* Helen Gardner, ed. Oxford, UK: Clarendon Press, 1970.

INDEX

Rick Friedman

A former professor of European History at Princeton University, Robert Darnton is Carl H. Pforzheimer University Professor and director of the Harvard University Library. The founder of the Gutenberg-e program, he is the author of many books. He lives in Cambridge, Massachusetts.

PublicAffairs is a publishing house founded in 1997. It is a tribute to the standards, values, and flair of three persons who have served as mentors to countless reporters, writers, editors, and book people of all kinds, including me.

I. F. STONE, proprietor of *I. F. Stone's Weekly*, combined a commitment to the First Amendment with entrepreneurial zeal and reporting skill and became one of the great independent journalists in American history. At the age of eighty, Izzy published *The Trial of Socrates*, which was a national bestseller. He wrote the book after he taught himself ancient Greek.

BENJAMIN C. BRADLEE was for nearly thirty years the charismatic editorial leader of *The Washington Post*. It was Ben who gave the *Post* the range and courage to pursue such historic issues as Watergate. He supported his reporters with a tenacity that made them fearless and it is no accident that so many became authors of influential, best-selling books.

ROBERT L. BERNSTEIN, the chief executive of Random House for more than a quarter century, guided one of the nation's premier publishing houses. Bob was personally responsible for many books of political dissent and argument that challenged tyranny around the globe. He is also the founder and longtime chair of Human Rights Watch, one of the most respected human rights organizations in the world.

. . .

For fifty years, the banner of Public Affairs Press was carried by its owner Morris B. Schnapper, who published Gandhi, Nasser, Toynbee, Truman, and about 1,500 other authors. In 1983, Schnapper was described by *The Washington Post* as "a redoubtable gadfly." His legacy will endure in the books to come.

Peter Osnos, *Founder and Editor-at-Large*